MW01241530

PowerAchieving

*Learn how to turn the potential
that exists inside of you into reality.*

J.T. Stewart

Achievement Publishing Group
P.O. Box 340432
Dayton, Ohio 45434

www.powerachievers.com

PowerAchieving: Turning your potential into reality.

Copyright 2002 by J.T. Stewart.

For more information contact:
J.T. Stewart Enterprises, Inc.
P.O. Box 340432
Dayton, Ohio 45434
1-800-379-2871

PowerAchieving may be purchased for educational, business, or sales promotion use. To purchase this book in bulk contact:

Special Markets Department
J. Thomas Group
P.O. Box 340432
Dayton, Ohio 45434
jthomasgrp@aol.com
First Edition

Cover design by Don Massie Designs,don@graphicdirections.com

ISBN: 0-9718541-0-6

Table of Contents

Dedication

This book is a work that has evolved through the years. It has been evolving through good times and bad times. Life is like that you know. It is dedicated to Tom and Ethel, the greatest parents that a little boy ever could have. They taught through example and were always there to encourage when the odds against achieving seemed great. To Princess Ruthann who always believed. You are the best. To David Heath wherever you are, for taking the time to teach a misguided teenager more than drama; you taught life. To Chris Haller, God rest his soul. You, Chris my man, were a true brother. I miss you. Thanks Leon for letting me share Saturdays with Team Corvette. Most of all, this book is dedicated to the Lord. Even though I sometimes fail him, he is always there. Thank you Lord.

About the Author

J.T. Stewart is a top success coach and speaker. As the president of J. Thomas Group, a marketing and public relations firm, J.T. has gained exposure for clients on programs such as Good Morning America, 20/20, Moneyline with Lou Dobbs, and The O'Reilly Factor. J.T. has written for and gained client exposure in USA Today, The Wall Street Journal, Newsweek and many more top publications. J.T. has been a successful businessperson for over 20 years. Mr. Stewart is the founder of PowerAchievers.com and has been involved in land development projects as a principal in Smash Development, a land development company. Mr. Stewart served as the president of the entertainment firm Smash Productions. J.T. Stewart was a founding partner in a speaker's bureau that grew over five hundred percent in sales in four years. J.T. Stewart can be heard as the host of "The J.T. Stewart Show" on Cox Broadcasting station WHIO-AM in Dayton, Ohio and as the host of "PowerAchieving Today", a syndicated radio show on the PowerAchievers Radio Network. J.T. Stewart's passion is helping others turn their "potential" into "reality" through speaking and writing.

Forward

If you are an underachiever, you are in trouble. In a world that moves faster with each keystroke, if you are an overachiever, you are barely keeping up. You need a new strategy. That strategy is PowerAchieving. PowerAchieving is not your typical "success" book. It is more. PowerAchieving is about the journey we take as we become successful. PowerAchieving reveals details on how to get where we want to go. It is a guide for that journey. This book will allow you to see life and the Powers that control your life in a new way. PowerAchieving is filled with real strategies that will help you on the hike to the top of the mountain. This is a very personal book. PowerAchieving is about YOUR success and achieving the things YOU want in life. Unlike many contests in life and in business, PowerAchieving does not make you compete against others. Usually when there is a contest, there is a loser. We have been conditioned to believe this because when the contest is over, we congratulate the winner and give them a prize. I believe there are no losers in life. Some just win to a lesser degree. Whether it is a sporting event or perhaps a sales contest, the winner is put up on a pedestal and we say that they are great. I have been involved in sales promotions where maybe two or three people really try and the other ten just plug along. Was the winner of that contest truly great or were the other people they were competing against that bad?

PowerAchieving will help drive you to success by matching you up against yourself. You are competing against yourself. Only when you compete against yourself can you push yourself to be the very best. PowerAchieving is about you. Only you can be responsible for your own talent. Only you can be accountable for your own actions. Only you can control your own work ethic. If you are in a race and pay more attention to the others around you in the race, you will be distracted and run slower. If you are focused on the other people in the race, you are not free to run your own race. There is a phrase in sports that carries over into life. It is *play within yourself*. This means use the talents that God gave you to do what you do best. Don't try to hit home runs if you are not a power hitter. Do what you do best. You are the best "you" there will ever be. You are the ONLY you there will ever be. PowerAchieving lays a foundation and then reveals powers that will help you achieve the things you want. PowerAchieving focuses on you and how to turn your potential into reality. It is hard to cash potential at the bank. You have a richness inside of you that will continue to be a hidden treasure unless you discover it. Once you discover it, you must then use it to make your life the most awesome journey that a person can take. It is your life. Live it to the fullest by turning your potential into reality.

Acknowledgements

What others say about PowerAchieving

"J.T. Stewart has tapped into what helps a person achieve their dreams. PowerAchieving comes from within. This book is a guide for the journey of success. In three words—It is exciting!!"

—Bill Havens, *professional speaker and the former "Mr. Clean"*

"Awesome, powerful, inspiring, moving, challenging, life changing. J.T. Stewart's humorous real-life tales make him one of the greatest storytellers and motivators of our time. Reading this book will give anyone, at any age, in any profession, the ability to become a PowerAchiever."

—Annie Matheson
Award Winning Sales Executive
Mcleod USA

1
What is PowerAchieving?

Imagine if you will, you are on a beach with beautiful white sand, waves crashing onto the shore, the warm sun radiating down. Your body soaks up the warm rays of the natural sunlight, the gentle breeze cools you as you sip a cold fruit drink. Your only thought is to relax. Ahhhh, peace. Do you feel it? Can you visualize it? Can you feel the sun as it wraps itself around your body? Can you see the waves as they break onto the shore? Take a moment to allow yourself to feel it, visualize it. Doesn't this sound and feel great? It does if you are in a cold winter climate. Doesn't it make you want to get on an airplane and go? Palm trees, sand, sun. Ahhhh...paradise. Now, how are you going to get there?

Some people simply pick up the phone and make the reservations and pay for it on their credit cards or write a check. Others don't have that luxury. They may not have the money to go. They may not have the time. They might have to find someone to watch the kids. They might have to take a second job to save the money. They want to go on this trip with all of their heart but their mountain is a little steeper to climb. Their obstacles are a little bigger. Their circumstances may not be the best. The gulf between potential and reality is a little wider for them. The gulf is wider and the journey will be more of a struggle than perhaps those around them. They can achieve it but they will need a new and better strategy. The new strategy is called PowerAchieving.

Through this book, I want to help you turn your potential into a reality. I want to help you achieve more than you ever thought you could. I want to take you beyond achieving. I want to take you to a higher level of achievement. I want to help you PowerAchieve. PowerAchieving goes beyond achieving. PowerAchieving is achieving even when you face the greatest of odds, odds that seem insurmountable. When you face great odds or you have a little higher mountain to climb than the next person, you must create a different plan. When your mountain is a little steeper, it takes a better strategy to get you there. If you were going to climb Pikes Peak, you would need one plan, but if you were going to climb Mount Everest, you would need another plan all together. PowerAchieving is designed to help you climb the Mount Everest's in your life. There is a big difference between just achieving and PowerAchieving.

Webster's definition of achieving is, "to perform, accomplish, to gain: to win." What is a PowerAchiever? The definition of PowerAchieving is, "*achieving extraordinary results from less than ordinary circumstances.*" PowerAchieving is not based on just where you end up. PowerAchieving takes into account where you start and then end up. PowerAchieving is not about just making money. PowerAchieving is about being happy in who you are. PowerAchieving deals with your personal richness, not just riches. PowerAchieving is for your total life.

Here is an example. If a person with a net worth of one million dollars invests their money into a new business and creates a profit, we would say that that person has achieved great wealth which is true; however, take a single mother of two who, after her husband left, paying no child support, goes on welfare and works a job. She gets off of welfare, moves from government assisted housing to an apartment, gets a job promotion, saves enough for a down payment on a house, improves her education, works hard, gets another promotion and is now moving into a middle class tax bracket. She is a "PowerAchiever".

PowerAchieving: Achieving Extraordinary Results From Less Than Ordinary Circumstances

I was speaking at a private club last year and after my talk, a nicely dressed woman asked to speak to me. She said, "Remember what you said about the woman on welfare? Well that was me. My husband left me and took everything except the kids. I ended up on welfare." She then seemed to get lost in her thoughts and with a tone of voice that sounded part desperate and part angry she said, "and I hated it." Her eyes dropped to the floor as she recounted her story. "I moved back to Ohio, got a job as a sales person, and now I am sales manager," she said. "I guess that makes me a PowerAchiever." Cheryl Waltz was a living example of what a PowerAchiever is.

Her mountain was a little steeper to climb. Her odds of success were a little longer than other people's. When the odds are long and you don't think it can be done, when they tell you it will never work, a PowerAchiever does it anyway. PowerAchieving: *achieving extraordinary results from less than ordinary circumstances*.

In your life, you have most likely had some less than ordinary circumstances that have confronted you. You have come against some obstacles that, at first glance, seem insurmountable. Maybe you have some of those obstacles in your life right now. These obstacles or barriers are like huge mountains in front of us. We must figure out how to get over these mountains and reach the other side. These life mountains can cause our life to take strange twists and turns. Just as when you drive through the mountains on vacation the road is not always straight, sometimes the road goes over the mountains, sometimes there is a tunnel that leads through the mountain, but most of the time the road twists and turns around the mountain with steep grades and sharp turns. These roads, if navigated carelessly, can cause danger. Your life mountains must be navigated with care and caution as well, if you are to avoid the dangers that lie ahead.

What are some of the obstacles that block your path to achieving the things you want? What mountains do you have in front of you that stand in the way of your achieving all that you desire? What mountain must you climb so you can reach the beach that waits for you on the other side? There are no mountains that you cannot climb. Mountains look big when you are at the bottom looking up. You can look at them as a challenge, or you can look at them as an obstacle. It all depends on your view. If your mountains look too big, then change how you look at them. Change your view. View them as a challenge, not an obstacle.

There Are No Mountains That You Cannot Climb

I want to show you how those less than ordinary circumstances can be overcome so you can produce exceptional results. You can "PowerAchieve". I want to help you identify the obstacles and then help you overcome them. If a builder were going to build a great building, he would have to lay down a strong foundation. If you are going to build a great life for yourself, you must also start with a strong foundation. PowerAchieving starts with a solid foundation. On top of that foundation is then placed building blocks consisting of different "Powers" that will make your life strong.

The foundation to PowerAchieving is made up of three elements. These elements are:

- **Vision**
- **Creativity**
- **Resiliency**

This foundation will help you build wealth, but more than wealth, this foundation and the following "Powers" will help you create personal richness. Wealth is great but what good is it to gain the whole world and lose one's soul? What good is it to lose one's self by not being true to yourself? What good is it to be rich on the outside but poor and unhappy on the inside? With money comes responsibility. Many people live to get the almighty dollar but they have no life. I believe that you can have both. You can have wealth and happiness. You can achieve the life that you want. You can make your vision a reality. You can PowerAchieve beyond your wildest imagination. You can be happy in your relationships. You can be financially secure. You can have the things you want. Today is the start of your journey to PowerAchieving. Don't you dare settle for second best. You deserve to have the life you have always wanted. Why not you? This is your life. Take control. Take control right now. Start today. Don't settle for just achieving. Climb your highest mountains. PowerAchieve. There is a place in the back of each chapter to write notes. There will be thoughts that will come to you that you will want to jot down for later use. Get a highlight pen and highlight thoughts that strike a cord with you as you read. Be involved in this book. This book is for you.

This Is Your Life—Take Control

"Power" Page

Use this page to write your thoughts.
List the areas of your life that you can control.

2
Vision

I want to explore the three elements that make up the foundation of PowerAchieving. The three elements are: VISION, CREATIVITY, and RESILIENCY. Let's get started by taking a look at VISION.

Have you ever set out to achieve something only to fall short of your goal? Any speaker or trainer worth a cup of coffee has repeated for years that you have got to have goals. Businesses have their employees list or write down their goals. "Your goal is to sell 100 widgets this month" or "Our goal is to do one million in sales this month." I believe in setting goals. I believe in writing your goals down. Everything that we have learned about goals I buy into 100%; however, I believe that we have missed the most critical foundation or prelude to goal setting—VISION.

I like to explain it like this; a vision is when you, in your mind, see yourself driving that BMW or other fine car. You see the picture in your mind. You see what color it is and what kind of wheels it has. You see yourself at the stoplight in the BMW. You see yourself driving it down a country road. You actually visualize yourself in that car. You don't just dream about having a new BMW someday, you actually visualize yourself specifically driving that car. When I asked you to visualize being on the beach I didn't say, "Think about being on vacation on some beach." I said visualize "the warm sun, the waves crashing, feel the cool breeze as you sip a cold fruit drink." Please don't get visions and dreams confused.

A dream is general. A vision is specific. Dreams are good, but many times we don't put action with our dreams. Dreams tend to be thought of as "someday". "Someday I want to be rich." "Someday I want a big house." "Someday I want to go to Hawaii." A dream is the seed that grows into a vision. It is important to dream but don't stop there. Let that dream grow into a vision. A vision is more focused. A dream is when you see the beach in Hawaii. A vision is when you see yourself on that beach in Hawaii. *A vision allows you to believe it is possible because you see yourself doing it.* In the movies or on television when the actors have a dream sequence, the screen goes out of focus and they play the "dream" music with a harp. The dream in television or movies is out of focus. Dreams in real life are out of focus as well. A vision is a dream that is focused. The vision is the true foundation of a goal.

A Dream Is General—A Vision Is Specific

A goal is the next step in this process of achieving your desires. A goal demands action. The goal process begins when you start taking action by saving your money to make the down payment to purchase the BMW. The goal starts when you start saving a hundred dollars a month for twelve months until you have the down payment. Goals are born from a vision. Goals are systematic steps taken toward the vision. Goals should be driven by a vision. Most people have dreams but they don't sharpen those dreams into a specific vision. They dream of "someday" but don't go any further because dreams are built on hopes, and visions are built on desire. Goals are built on action. A vision is personal. There is a difference. Before there is a goal, there must be a vision.

Every January 1st millions of people wipe the slate clean and start the year with a New Year's resolution. The most common New Year's resolution is, "I'm going to lose 50 lbs. and really get in shape," and another one is, "I am going to get organized and double my income." Why is it that so many people make New Year's resolutions and can't keep them? Why do so many people set their goals, maybe even write them down, but don't achieve them? It is because there is no vision. They have skipped ahead to goal setting without a true vision. There is no specific plan because there is no specific vision. They don't visualize themselves a hundred pounds thinner so there is no passion for the goal because they don't really believe that they can do it anyway. So they don't do it. They give up. It is like trying to drive a car with no gas. We know where we want to go but don't have the necessary fuel to get there. Having a vision will spark passion. Passion is the fuel that drives the goal process. Without the proper fuel, people "run out of gas" before they reach their goal.

A true vision comes from the soul and is processed through the mind and creates a fantastic series of events. A vision that is true creates a passion, and that passion creates drive, and that drive is what creates the results. Let me say that again. This is a great formula for achieving all that you desire. A vision that is created from the soul will cause a chain reaction of success. Are you ready? Here we go. I repeat. A vision creates passion. Passion is the fuel that creates the drive. Nothing of greatness has ever been achieved without passion. The passion creates the drive. A person who has a great passion will be driven to work. A person with a vision has such passion that they become driven to achieve. A person with passion is driven to get out of bed early and stay on the job a little later. When you are driven by a vision and passion, you will get results.

A Vision Creates Passion, Passion Creates Drive, And Drive Creates Results

Do you have a vision? Where do you see yourself? What do you want out of life? The vision creates passion and passion creates drive and drive gets results. Are you achieving all that you want? Have you had a vision in the past but now you are in a very different place than you once envisioned? Are you settling for the hand life has dealt you? Perhaps you started out on this journey of life with a vision or dream and as you were faced with an obstacle or as you climbed over the mountain things changed. As you drove up the twisting winding mountain road, something happened and you either got lost or pulled off to the side. The road of life is filled with many parking places. Maybe you "ran out of gas." Perhaps you got tired, or for whatever reason you haven't made it over the mountain...YET!!!! Back out of that parking place and let's go. You still have the vision but it is not fresh. It is not a focused vision. Your vision now seems more like a dream that is far off and cloudy. Don't give up hope. Visualize your achievements and success. I CHALLENGE YOU...RENEW YOUR VISION!!!!

There was a flock of geese that were on the journey south for the winter and as they flew a few days, they landed at a farmer's pond to get a drink and rest. Well, the farmer just loved geese. He thought they were beautiful. He loved to watch them fly in a "V" formation. He loved to listen to them honk as they flew by. He was so excited that he went and got a bag of bread to feed the flock. The geese thought, "Hey, this is pretty good. Maybe we will just stay here tonight and eat the farmer's bread and drink from the pond." So they did. Before they left the next morning, the farmer brought another bag of bread to feed them. The geese thought, "Well, we better eat before we go." So they did. The geese felt so comfortable and were being taken care of so they thought, "Hey, let's just stay

18

here." So they did. They stopped so long and were so comfortable they forgot to go south and never returned north. They lost their vision and direction.

Being taken care of is not all bad, but at what expense? Do we give up our hopes and desires just to be comfortable? Some people would say "yes". The bottom third of the mountain of life is filled with the comfortable crowd. The higher you climb the mountain of life the less crowded it is. That is why very few people enjoy the spectacular view from the top. They all want to see the view from the top, but the journey is not comfortable enough for them. They abandon the journey and settle for comfort. When people do this, they short change themselves and rob themselves of their potential.

This can happen to us if we allow it. We can get comfortable and lose sight of where we were going. This happened to me. I had a vision to create a public relations firm, as well as further my speaking career. In the process, by chance, I ran into a former client who had become a good friend. We met and I ended up taking on a PR project for him. Little by little, the project became bigger, the money a little better, until I was pretty much a full-time employee. Pouring my effort into his project and taking the steady retainer, while fun, wasn't my vision.

I had sacrificed my vision because it was comfortable and steady. I still have this client, but I was smart enough to wake up and change our arrangement so I could focus on my vision. Are you like the geese? Have you settled? Have you compromised your vision? You don't have to. Never let go of your vision. The bible, which is the greatest motivational book ever, says, "Without a vision the people will perish." They don't die physically, but perish in their heart. They become depressed and unhappy from the inside.

Without A Vision The People Perish

Have you ever seen a depressed person who has a vision and/or is working on their goals? No, they don't have time to be depressed. When you look to the horizon, it will force you to keep your head up. If you have someplace to go, you don't have time to stop and wallow in the pigpen of self-pity. You have a vision and you are on a journey to get there. Many great athletes know the importance of having a vision. When Tiger Woods won the Masters, he said, "Coming up the 18th green was better than I envisioned." When Terrell Davis, the all-pro running back of the Denver Broncos was named Super Bowl's most valuable player, he said, "It is better in person than in my vision." Jack Nicholas envisions each hole of the golf course, each shot, before he plays a tournament. He has a vision of winning. Grammy award winning singer Faith Hill, said in a recent interview that she knew music would take her somewhere; she had a vision of it.

What is your vision? Your life is about your vision. Do not settle. Shakespeare said, "All the world is a stage and we are the players." He was right; as our life plays out, we realize that this is not a dress rehearsal. It is very easy to lose sight of our vision if we are not careful. Keep your vision the main focus. The main thing is to keep the main thing, the main thing. Concentrate on and stay true to your vision. You can stop and smell the roses, just don't take up gardening. In the "Power Page" section in the back of this chapter, write down your vision. What do you want to be and do? What really makes you want to jump out of bed and go to it? Keep your vision focused. What do you visualize yourself doing? Perhaps you have had a vision of being a singer. Visualize yourself on that stage. Perhaps you want a bigger house. Visualize that house. See yourself in that house. Write in detail. If you are a singer, where are you performing? If you want to own your own business, where is it? What does your office look like?

Dream in black and white but visualize in color. If you are going to see your vision into reality, it is going to take effort. *Don't let your effort be less than your vision.*

Your Life Is About Your Vision

"Power" Page

Write your vision in detail.

3
Creativity

The second element of PowerAchieving is CREATIVITY. Once you have a vision of what you want and where you want to be in life, you must then take concrete steps to arrive at your destination. You are going to have to be creative to get there. Success and creativity are very much akin to one another. When the odds are stacked against you and others around you, family, friends and doubters tell you that you can't do it. They tell you it can't be done. It is because they don't see all of the angles that can be used to attack the problem. They only see the mountain in front of you. They don't see the many ways around that mountain.

A perfect example of being creative is when two brothers from my hometown of Dayton, Ohio, Orville and Wilber Wright, became the original PowerAchievers. When they started working on their flying machine, people thought they were absolutely nuts. No one had ever flown before, so people were laughing themselves silly when a couple of guys who owned a bicycle shop came up with this hair-brained idea. Can you imagine the talk around town? These guys have lost it! But they had all of the elements of PowerAchieving. First, they had a vision. Second, they were creative and innovative in how they attacked the problems they faced in making that vision a reality. Third, they were resilient. They tried it again and again when it didn't go well, until that famous day in Kitty Hawk, North Carolina when, for the first time ever, man flew with the birds and the world was changed forever.

How can your dreams change your world forever? Make your dreams into a specific vision. Think of some creative ways that you can use to make your vision come alive. Don't be afraid to dream. Dreaming is a creative process. People say, "I'm not a creative person." If you dream, you are creative. People say, "I don't believe in dreams." If we don't believe in dreams, why then do we fear nightmares? Dream big, but then focus that dream into a vision. The Wright Brothers did not just dream of flying, they took the dream and made it into a vision and then they used their creativity to turn that vision into reality.

To achieve your vision, your desires and your goals, you are going to call upon your creativity to solve problems and overcome obstacles. There is something powerful about looking at an obstacle or problem and saying, "Yes! I can overcome that." The great thing about creativity is there are no rules. Think outside of the box, it's okay. Anything goes.

Thinking outside of the box reminds me of a story that my good friend and comedian Mark Klein told me. Mark is one of the country's top comedians. He has been featured in GQ magazine and has been on 60 Minutes. Mark has carved quite a niche out for himself in the corporate world as the top comedian for corporate events. He is called the "Corp Jester." Mark tells the story about a group of investors that bought a racehorse at a claiming race for $500. A week later the horse dies. "What do we do now?" they said. The stable boy said, "I will get your money back and more." How? "Leave it to me," he said. "We will raffle off the horse." "You can't raffle off a dead horse," the investors cried. "Leave everything to me," said the stable boy. The stable boy had raffle tickets made up, "Race Horse Raffle - $50.00 per Chance." He sold 200 chances for $10,000, a $9,500 profit. He took the money to the owners. They were amazed. "Weren't the people mad when they found out the horse was dead?" they asked. The stable boy said, "Just the guy who won...but I gave his money back." That is a creative solution to a problem.

What are some creative ways to achieve your dreams and make your vision a reality? In our quest to move forward with our vision, we come up against many obstacles. If we take the standard road that everyone else takes, we will limit ourselves to the average crowd. You are better than average.

Imagine if you were going to the hospital for an emergency and you had to get there in a hurry but there was a traffic jam. Would you just move along at a snails pace following the car in front of you or would you find a faster way to the hospital? Would you find a side street, or a different route? Sure you would, because there is an emergency. People do some creative driving when they are in a situation like that. Is your life any less urgent? Don't follow the crowd. This is your life. Creativity to conquer a problem takes action. Ideas are a dime a dozen; people who put them into action are priceless.

Think Outside Of The Box

A real life example of using creativity to overcome a problem or obstacle and achieving success is when I had a public relations client who wanted to be featured in the ABC News Show, 20/20. My client owned a very interesting business. He conducted undercover drug investigations inside of corporations. Charles Carroll, the C.E.O. of the A.S.E.T. corporation, knew if he could expose what his undercover agents were seeing inside of companies across the nation, that other companies would look to his firm to help them get rid of drug use and he would get more business. This is a great strategy. When other C.E.O.'s look at the losses that a company takes because of drug abuse, it is overwhelming and they often take action after they are educated. Mr. Carroll wanted to use 20/20 to help educate and expose the problem. There was one little problem, I was in Dayton, Ohio, not exactly the media capital of the world, and 20/20 was in New York.

I worked for about 6 months trying to pitch the idea to 20/20. After working my way up the food chain, I found out that a lady named Jamie Zahn was the one who decided what got on the air. I called her. Her receptionist was less than warm. I sent information. No reply. I followed up. Miss Zahn was always too busy to talk. I left voice mail. Never returned. I just was not getting anywhere, so I decided to send her a gift. Not just any gift. My client had what is called a video print, which is a picture much like a Polaroid taken from video surveillance footage.

I took a video print of a suspect snorting cocaine on the job and put it in a very nice frame and Fed Ex-ed it to her with a letter that said, "This is a portrait of America's workforce". The letter said, "These are the people who make the brakes that go on busses that take your kids to school. Feel free to keep the frame and as you place a picture of a loved one in it, please remember…" I then gave her statistics on drug abuse in the workplace. Well, guess who called. That's right. Jamie Zahn. Michael Pressman a 20/20 producer flew in from New York and six weeks later my client was on 20/20. Sometimes you will have to achieve through creativity. When being creative, you are going to have to do things that have perhaps never been done before. Never be afraid to try something new. Be creative in overcoming your obstacles. Your vision and dreams are worth it.

Amateurs Built The Ark; Professionals Built The Titanic

"Power" Page

List a problem that you currently face
and then write a creative solution to it.
Don't be afraid to think outside of the box.

4
Resiliency

The third element of PowerAchieving is RESILIENCY. We must be able to bounce back when things do not go our way. You cannot look behind you and move forward. Things in this life will not always go our way. There are going to be times of great disappointment. You may suffer personal or financial loss. Understand that in our life, we will experience setbacks. The real key to overcoming the setbacks is keeping your eyes on the vision or goal. Don't focus on the negative. If you "stare" at the negative you will never "see" the positive. Keeping your head up forces you to look ahead. It takes courage to be resilient. It takes courage to get up and move ahead when life has dealt us an unbelievable blow. Life has a way of trying us through fire. You do not go through the fire without actually going through the fire. You will feel the heat. It will be uncomfortable. It will hurt. There will be pain. But you must have the courage, when life knocks you down, to get up. Keep going. Thomas Edison, when inventing the light bulb, never gave up and never thought of failure. Instead of accepting failure he said, "I have not failed, I have successfully found 10,000 ways that this won't work." Resiliency. Being resilient is about accepting the negative thing that has happened and then moving on. Forget it and move forward. The past is the past. If you continue to live in the past, your life is history. You must get up and move on.

Are you holding on to baggage from the past that is weighing you down on your journey into the future? If so, go ahead and unpack.

Success is being able to go from failure to failure without losing enthusiasm. With every opportunity, there is opposition. A big shot is just a little shot that kept on shooting. The ammunition that allows us to keep shooting is a positive attitude. A healthy, balanced positive attitude allows us to keep going when we would rather not. Setbacks are an exercise in toughness. Setbacks separate our desires from our wants. Think about that! If we want something and encounter a setback or an obstacle, many times we will change our wants. We don't want it as bad as we thought. But our desires are a little different.

It Takes Courage To Get Up And Move Ahead

If you truly desire something, you will expend more effort. You will try harder. You will be stronger. This will happen because a desire is deeper. A desire is more personal than a want. Desires come from the heart. With every opportunity comes opposition. Expect opposition. You know opposition is going to come, so be prepared. Things are easier to deal with when you know they are coming. If you have a vision that is personal and true to you, it becomes a desire. It will be harder to be knocked down by a setback when we are trying to achieve our desires.

Opposition comes in many forms. You may get opposition from co-workers, the boss, family, even yourself. The person most likely to steal your dreams is...you. Believe it. How many times have you talked yourself out of doing something by saying things like, "I don't deserve that," or "I can't just walk up there and talk to that person." Negative thoughts lead to negative action. You have total control of achieving your vision. Don't doubt yourself. If you really believe in your vision, your desires, then you must focus on the opportunity, not the roadblocks. You cannot let the negative opposition dominate your thoughts and time. Nobody is going to say that this life is easy. The journey is going to get tough. Your desire will determine your resiliency.

Mark Hild graduated from Tecumseh High School in 1990. Since the tender age of 8 years old, Mark has been fighting the most deadly form of Muscular Dystrophy. Mark's desire and vision was to complete his higher education and earn his college degree. But Mark's dream was becoming less and less of a reality. Mark spent more and more time in the hospital as his Muscular Dystrophy got worse and worse. Countless times Mark went to the hospital to fight pneumonia and other illnesses associated with muscular dystrophy. Each time Mark got out of the hospital, he exercised the power of resiliency and took another step toward his dream of a college degree. It took 10 years! It took a decade of staying with it. Mark Hild received his degree from Wright State University. As Mark spoke at the commencement to his fellow students, many of whom were in grade school when Mark started his college life, Mark Hild said, "If I can overcome to succeed, so can you."

Focus On The Opportunity, Not The Roadblocks

Have you given up on your dream, your desires? Do you still close your eyes and visualize your future? Have you allowed the negative forces in your life to steal your dreams? Has a setback or failure caused you to take a seat on the bench in this game of life? Are you settling for second best or second choice? You cannot allow the setbacks to make you give up. DON'T EVER GIVE UP!!

Shakespeare said, "All the world is a stage and we are the players." That is true. We all play a role in this big show we call life. Some are moms and dads, some are doctors, policemen, and factory workers. There are many roles in this show. You get up each morning and put on your costume and go to work and play the part. You come home at the end of the day and your role changes. It is true, *all the world is a stage and we are the players*, but this is NOT dress rehearsal. This is the big show. It is happening now. You are on! This is the theater of life. You are the star. There is power in being resilient.

The power of resiliency reminds me of a ballet performance by the Dayton Ballet Company. The curtain was raised and the skilled dancers appeared in wonderful costumes. They were strong and powerful as they glided across the stage. They danced with such grace. Each choreographed move was executed with precision. The performance was a thing of beauty…and then the unthinkable happened, one of the dancers fell. The gasp of the audience was deafening. The dancer got up and continued, but it happened again to another dancer, then again. An incredible 17 falls. It seems the problem was the fog machine that they were using to create an effect was creating a thin coat of slick moisture on the stage. The moisture was causing the dancers to fall. Isn't that just like life? We are moving along through life. Everything seems so perfect, so planned, so choreographed and then, without warning, something happens and we fall. We lose a job or make a bad financial move. Maybe a relationship breaks up. It seems the whole world is watching. We are embarrassed. It hurts. The only thing to do is get back up, dust ourselves off and keep going. The show must go on. Life must go on. It doesn't mean that there is not pain or hurt when we fall. There will be. The real pain comes when you don't get up.

The feelings that go along with falling are fear, embarrassment, surprise, hurt, and doubt. All are natural emotions and feelings. You can overcome those emotions by being resilient and getting up. There is incredible power in getting up. The emotions of getting up are confidence, bravery, and focus. When things don't go your way and you experience a setback, you need to then experience a bounce back. The ballet dancers were not all of a sudden a bunch of klutzes. They still possessed the same great talent and skill. They just had a bad circumstance. Because you have experienced a setback doesn't mean that you are less talented or less of a person. It means you went through a tough situation. The only way that a particular situation can cause you harm is if you don't get up and exercise the power of resiliency.

You belong to the power that you obey. Many people get knocked off course or have their dreams taken away because a setback happens. Setbacks are a part of life. They will happen. When a setback happens, the majority of people don't get back up, they make excuses. They now have an excuse to help them fail instead of getting up and moving forward. There is a difference between failing and being a failure. Failing can many times be a stepping stone to bigger things. A failure is a person who fails at something and then gives up. Excuses are what losers use to be failures. Resiliency is what you use to become a winner. If a football player didn't get up after they were tackled, they would never reach the goal line. If you don't get up when life tackles you, then you will never reach your personal goal line. The power of resiliency is essential if you are going to reach your personal goal line.

You Belong To The Power That You Obey

The elements or foundation of PowerAchieving do not necessitate that we do things faster and our life become more intense. Actually, it is the opposite. There is more to life than increasing it's speed. In a world that gets faster with each keystroke, PowerAchieving is designed to help you achieve more with less stress. The three elements: vision, creativity and resiliency are designed to be positive components of a positive process. Each one is forward thinking. Vision is a positive element that demands an innermost desire be fulfilled. As you focus on the vision, it blocks out unnecessary distractions and allows positive thoughts to dominate. Creativity releases endorphins into our brain and creates positive actions such as laughter. Creativity reduces stress and releases positive endorphins that suppress stress hormones.

Resiliency helps us to refocus on our vision, which puts us back in the positive state that we need to PowerAchieve. Vision, Creativity, and resiliency form the foundation to PowerAchieving.

"Power" Page

What obstacles do you have to overcome
to achieve your vision? Write them here.

5
"The Power of You"

There are many forces that work in our lives to make things happen. There are many powers. When we understand these powers, we can manage them to help us achieve our dreams.

Perhaps the most significant power is also the most basic power. It is the "Power of You". I don't mean power in a negative way. I mean power as in control and responsibility—positive power. I am talking about power that can help you control your life. You will not have power over every event that happens in your life, but the "Power of You" gives you control of how you handle those events in your life. I believe that a basic element that leaves people feeling powerless is the fact that many people, maybe you, don't truly, deep down inside, believe in themselves. That disbelief acts like a prison that keeps their happiness captive. That disbelief won't allow them to be free to move beyond fear. The disbelief in themselves acts like an invisible fence that is used to keep pets in a yard. When we get to the edge of our predetermined limits, limits that either we or someone else has placed on us, we get a little shock of fear and we go back to the middle of the yard where it is safe. We never believe that we are able to extend ourselves. What is your invisible fence? What keeps you from moving beyond the barriers that have been set?

The fact that most, and I do mean most people don't truly believe in themselves is indeed a drain on achieving our desires and reaching our vision. How can the "Power of You" work if you don't have confidence in you? I really believe that our self-esteem, how we feel about ourselves, is the key to achieving. The "Power of You" starts with you. If you don't love and value yourself, you will never be able to love and value others. I do a lot of motivational talks in schools and absolutely love it. I saw a great sign in a school hallway one day. It said, "I know I'm somebody, cause God don't make no junk." I believe that with all of my heart. You were created, born with value and purpose. You were born for a reason. We sometimes spend so much time "adding" up our troubles that we forget to "count" our blessings. I believe that man was created in God's image. You may or may not share the same belief. That is okay. I don't believe that you or I were created by mistake. Our parents might not have planned us, but we were not a mistake. God does not make mistakes. When you realize and understand that you are somebody, that is the first step to achieving. Without this understanding, the odds against achieving our dreams go up.

If You Don't Love And Value Yourself, You Will Never Be Able To Love And Value Others

I am an expert on self-esteem. Now, let me temper that statement by saying that at my age, I can look back and see in perfect hindsight how a lack of self-esteem affected my life. I was 3 lbs. 6 oz when I was born. That sounds bad. I was actually happy to be born. I was full term. In those days…ah…1958, modern technology did not exist. They never thought I would make it through the night. They wouldn't even let my mother see me. She sneaked down in the middle of the night to look for me. They wouldn't even tell her if I was alive. They put me in an incubator and an iron lung for 6 weeks. One doctor suggested letting me die because I would never be like other kids. They were right! I'm not like others. I'm unique...and so are you!! Growing up without actually physically growing was tough. I was a 50 pound 5th grader and literally played football as a sophomore weighing in at a massive 98 pounds. At my football physical, the high school football coaches had to go to the elementary school to find me a football helmet. It was still big.

Can you imagine being the smallest kid in school? Not the smallest boy, the smallest kid, period. At recess the big kids would pick teams and after everyone was chosen, girls included, there I was, alone, standing against the fence, the last one picked, the one nobody wanted. I knew this because the big kids were fighting over me, "You take him," and "No, you take him." Wow! What a way to build a kid's self esteem. It is bad enough to go through those awkward junior high years, but try being in junior high in a fifth grader's body. Even the nerds picked on me.

I played little league baseball and I was the littlest of the little leaguers. I put the word "little" in little league. I never got a hit in little league. Nobody could pitch to me. I was a sure base on balls every time. They walked me every time. If you have ever seen the movie "Simon Birch," you know what I mean. My mother always said I would have a growth spurt. I am still waiting. I am not bemoaning the fact that I am short. In fact, I had a dream a few years ago that I drank a drink and grew to over 6 feet tall. I woke up in a panic. I didn't want to be six feet tall. I liked me the way I was. Being short has shaped who I am and forced me to overlook what many people consider a "shortcoming".

Funny thing, I really never think of or see myself as short. The only time I do is when I see a photo of myself with a taller person. How you see yourself will determine how you act. I don't see myself as short so I don't act as if I am less of a person. I am not. If you place limits on yourself, you will never be able to release the "Power of You". It is not what is on the outside that matters; it is who you are on the inside that makes you who you are. How do you view yourself? Do you like what you see? We can certainly work to improve ourselves and our appearance. We can go to the gym, go on a diet, change our hairstyle; many things can be done to improve our outward appearance. If you feel like you need a new look—do it!! We can also make changes on the inside and become a better person by changing some of our habits and behaviors. Building a healthy self image really means that we have to do things and exhibit behaviors that you like and would want to find in a friend or a mate. If you could change anything about yourself what would you change? The good news is, you can change. That is the "Power of You".

How You See Yourself Will Determine How You Act

The great thing about the "Power of You" is, you have the control to become the person you want to be. You can look at who you are and say, "I like this about me" or "I want to be more...kind, giving, thoughtful" or whatever. You can add or subtract behaviors in your life. The more positive behaviors you add to your life, the better you will feel about yourself. The better you feel about yourself, the more others gravitate to you and the more opportunities there are to use the "Power of You". It is a circle of positiveness. The "Power of You" starts with confidence, blended with a concern for others. This combination allows you to feel good about yourself while helping others around you feel good about themselves as well.

Try this exercise: identify five behaviors that make you, you. Write them on the "Power Page" in the back of this chapter. There are many more behaviors, but let's take the top five. Are you kind, selfish, aggressive, passive, positive, negative, angry, honest, a giver or a taker? Once you have identified the top 5 behaviors, write them down. Now go through and ask yourself which of these behaviors are going to help me the most in achieving my desires, my vision and goals. Take the best behaviors and work on using them to be a larger part of your personality each day. Get rid of the behaviors that hold you back or keep you from achieving. Change those destructive habits by replacing them with new positive ones.

If you answered that you are negative, then work on becoming more positive. The power to change is controlled by the "Power of You". If you don't like the direction you are heading, the "Power of You" allows you to make a "you" turn. That is the great thing about the "Power of You"—you have a say in your future and how you get there. Understand that you can achieve anything you want if you are willing to take an inventory of your emotions, behaviors and habits, and are willing to throw out those emotions, behaviors and habits that keep you from achieving and add those behaviors, habits, emotions and actions that help achieve.

The "Power Of You" Starts With Confidence Blended With A Concern For Others

The number one emotion that keeps people from achieving is fear. Fear is a natural emotion but it does not have to be a dream killer. I talk to people who want to follow their desires, hopes and visions but fear overcomes them and they let fear steal their desires and visions.

I do a great deal of work in the entertainment industry. A friend who was a singer at a local club gave me a demo tape of his girlfriend to see what I thought. She sang at weddings and small functions but not in clubs or big events. Debbie could really sing. Some people can sing and some people have the gift. Debbie had the gift, period. She was awesome. I was riding in my car and had the tape in the tape player when my passenger finally spoke up and said, "Who is this, Trisha Yearwood?" I said, "You will never guess who this is." After she had a few wrong guesses I said, "Debbie." "What!" "Yep, that is Darrell's girlfriend." "WOW, she can sing!" I took the tape with me to Nashville on a business trip. I went to visit my friends Marvin and Ann of Ann Gillis Productions. They make movies. When I got to their office on music row they had left a note for me to join them across the street at a little lunch spot on the row called Sammy-B's. I joined them there. They were talking to a gentleman who was a record producer. During the conversation I asked him if he would listen to the tape. We went back to Ann's office and listened to the tape. After listening to three songs he asked, "What does she look like?" I said that she was nice looking about twenty-six years old. We listened some more and then he said, "She could get a record deal here. I'll help her."

I came back home and met with Debbie about moving to Nashville. Debbie was afraid to move. She made excuses about little things and why she couldn't move. One minute Debbie said all that she ever wanted to do was sing and she would do anything to make it happen. When the opportunity was presented to her, she was afraid to move. The fear that she had was so great that it robbed her of the opportunity to live a life-long ambition. No matter what I said, Debbie always had a reason why she couldn't move to the one place that could turn her potential into reality. Debbie let fear become a dream stealer. What a shame.

I know so many people who want to own their own business but are fearful that they can't do it. They don't want to give up the security of a full-time job. What are they really afraid of? I would be more fearful of working for someone else and letting him or her control my future. There is no job security. They could be laid off tomorrow. Fear stands for False Evidence Appears Real—F.E.A.R. In the movie, "Bandits", Bruce Willis robs a bank by putting a magic marker to the back of the bank guard's head. The guard thought that the marker was a gun. Had the guard known that it was a marker and not a gun, he would not have been fearful and would have pulled his own gun. The "Power of You" is greater than the power of fear. Please understand that. Fear seems dominant but you are stronger than fear.

A key way to conquer fear is to know the facts. Legend has it that Jesse James, the leader of the James Gang bank robbers from the Old West, was on the run from the law. In the sleepy little town of Bowersville, Ohio, a bounty hunter named Nick Sparks got the drop on Jesse as he slept by the campfire early one morning. With gun drawn, the bounty hunter ordered Jesse James to get up and put his hands up. The bounty hunter gave Jesse a choice; either he would shoot him or Jessie could jump off of a nearby cliff. Jesse weighed all of the facts by easing over to the cliff, hands still in the air, to see how far the drop was. To his amazement, there was an 8-foot drop to a ledge over the cliff before the big drop. He told the bounty hunter he would jump, and as soon as he said it, he did it. Jessie jumped over the cliff to his death...or so the bounty hunter thought. The bounty hunter rushed over to the edge of the cliff to look. He couldn't believe that the great Jesse James had jumped. As he leaned over the cliff, Jesse, who was standing on the ledge, hit the bounty hunter in the head with a large rock. The bounty hunter fell to the ledge. Jesse James tied the bounty hunter up with his own rope, climbed up the ledge and escaped. You can escape your fears when you know the facts. Weigh all of the options. Your hopeless situation may not be hopeless when you look at the facts.

Fear Seems Dominant But You Are Stronger Than Fear

There are other times on your journey to achieving when you must simply take a leap of faith. Sometimes we have to be brave enough to just do it. This does not happen all of the time but every once in awhile it will come into play. The first time I performed at a comedy club was one of those times.

I was in Nashville on business. I always thought I was pretty funny. I had been speaking for about seven years but never in a comedy club. I had never even been in a club. I called Zanies Comedy Club in Nashville to see if they had an open mic night. Open mic nights are where amateurs perform stand up comedy to sharpen their skills. The pleasant sounding girl on the other end of the phone explained that there was no open mic night but they were having a "White Mountain Wine Cooler Laugh-Off." I asked, "What's that?" She explained that it was a competition with a prize of ten thousand dollars. I said, "Sign me up!" I got to the club early to check it out. There were ten comics. They all seemed extremely tense. We drew numbers from a hat to see what order we would go in. I picked number one. That is good, I think. We each got five minutes to perform. A comic named "Killer Beaz" was the emcee. He warmed up the crowd and got them laughing and then he introduced me. I was rolling along great. People were laughing at my jokes and things were good. Until…I forgot what I was supposed to say next. I stood there for about ten seconds. The audience looked at me and I looked at them for what seemed an eternity. Talk about fear. I finally remembered what was next and kept going. I faced a fear that I had. I had always wanted to do stand up comedy, but was afraid. I had overcome the fear and now I had done it. I found out later that all of the comics were professional touring comedians. If I had known that fact, I might not have done it. I was in WAY over my head. Oh, by the way, I placed fifth out of ten. Not bad for my first time.

The saddest thing in the world is for you to take your dreams to the grave with you because you were afraid. I pray that Debbie doesn't take her gift of singing and dreams of performing with her to her grave. Fear is one emotion that will cause a person to do nothing. Doing nothing is deadly when it comes to achieving all that you want. Remove fear and doubt from your personality and replace them with knowledge and confidence. Whenever you face a situation that makes you fearful or afraid, load up on knowledge; get the facts. If your doctor ran some tests on you and told you to come in right away to go over the results, you might be a little nervous. "Why does he want to see me right away? What's wrong?" Your mind may think the worst, "Oh my God, I must have a tumor." Your mind runs wild with fear. When you get to the doctor's office you find out that he is going on vacation and wanted to see you now because he was going to be gone out of town! Getting the facts will give you confidence. *Subtracting fear and doubt and adding knowledge and confidence reshapes your personality and makes you more powerful.*

Replace the negative behaviors with positive powers. It increases the "Power of You". Replacing negative behaviors with positive powers is a process that is ongoing. If you want to break through the fear barrier, do something that you are afraid of, face your fears. Maybe you are afraid of riding roller coasters, or flying in an airplane. Face your fear, go ride a roller coaster or take a trip in an airplane. Start with little tasks that are fearful to you. As you overcome those fears, move on to bigger fears. As your victories over your fears mount, your confidence will increase and your fear will decrease. The "Power of You" overcoming your fear is awesome. When you master the "Power of You", you can achieve anything.

The "Power Of You" Is Greater Than The Power Of Fear

"Power" Page

List your fears and what you can do to overcome them.

6
The "Power of Others"

No person is an island unto himself or herself. If you are going to achieve your goals and make your vision a reality, there will be other people who will be involved. The "Power of Others" will come into play. The old saying, "it's who you know" is true. A truer statement is, "it's who knows you." Groups and businesses spend millions of dollars each year putting together networking functions. Developing and growing your personal network is vital if you are going to achieve. Developing your network is going to take effort and time. It is an investment into your future. I see so many networking events that are unsuccessful because they focus on exchanging business cards and not building relationships.

Hear me loud and clear—building your personal network is ALL about building relationships. It is not about just meeting someone at an after hours event and exchanging business cards. Building those relationships takes effort. The more effort you invest in a relationship, the more your personal network will grow and the more valuable it will become. The person that you are building a relationship with has a network that can be opened up to you as well. Your personal network will grow into infinity if you invest in it.

I grew my personal network in Nashville with one conversation. I now have many wonderful friends in Nashville, not just contacts. I was talking to a school administrator in Marion, Ohio, Jan Mizell, who hired me to do motivational programs for her high school students. I told Jan that I would like to perhaps move to Nashville. She gave me her cousin's name who was working as a public relations director for the Grand 'ol Opry. I talked to her cousin, Judy, on the phone and then took her to dinner on my next visit there. The relationship with Judy led me to a gentleman who used to work for Judy, Chuck Whitting. After developing a relationship with Chuck and sharing my vision over lunch, Chuck introduced me to Ann Gillis, a film producer in Nashville. Ann and her husband Marvin became great friends and I worked with them on some projects. Through Ann, I met Robin Taylor who works with record labels and songwriters. I developed a great relationship with Robin. We would meet for lunch, talk on the phone and help each other out on projects. Robin called me one day and told me she passed my name on to a fellow named Tom Hays who needed help marketing a new idea. Two weeks later I was in Nashville and met with Tom. I worked with Tom and his lovely wife, Susan, on their project and have two cherished friends who now live in Napa Valley. When I needed help selling a television show to a network, I called Tom and he introduced me to John Adkins who helped. I could go on and on, but you get the point. I have developed relationships with hundreds of great people. All because of one five minute conversation with Jan Mizell.

Building Your Personal Network Is All About Building Relationships

Do you remember, when I said that you would need to invest in your personal network? I do mean invest. It is amazing how people remember you when you give them more than a business card. After meeting a person at a networking event that you think you would want to include in your personal network, start the relationship building process by sending them a thank you card or appropriate gift. Perhaps you should invite them to lunch. Make sure you buy the lunch. It is improper to invite someone to lunch and not buy. The inviting party always buys. Start the process of relationship building. Find out what they are working on and how you can help them, how can you open up your network to them. Build a friendship. People do business with friends. The time and money you spend on lunches, cards and gifts will come back to you sooner rather than later.

Don't call upon your network only when you need something. Drop them an e-mail, or better yet, call them on the phone and spend a couple of minutes visiting with them. The visit doesn't have to be long, just a minute to see how they are doing. If you see their name in the paper, clip out the article and send it to them with a congratulatory note. The "Power of Others" is HUGE. Achieving without it is impossible. People are drawn to a positive attitude. Always have a positive attitude when meeting new friends and building your network. Be a giver. Give encouragement. It doesn't cost you anything but it will pay off big with your network. Give time. Volunteering is a great way to spend time with people and get to know them while working together for the same cause. The relationship building process is enhanced ten-fold when you volunteer. You can't volunteer for everything so pick and choose carefully or you will be on every committee and board in town. Giving your time is a wise investment. We will talk about the power of giving later, but if you want the "Power of Others" to work for you, incorporate giving into your relationship-building and personal network.

People Do Business With Friends

"Power" Page

List twenty people that you have not had
contact with for over 6 months. Then send them a card.

7
The "Higher Power"

There is a third power in this trilogy of powers, The "Power of You", The "Power of Others" and the "Higher Power". There is an incredible peace knowing that we are not alone in this journey we call life. I was riding in a friend's new car and it had all of the latest gadgets and toys. We are talking about some serious bells and whistles. He could actually push a button and a voice would come on and give him directions, make phone calls, whatever he needed. It's called On-Star. It is a global positioning satellite. When he pushes a button, a signal is sent way up in space and then it is directed back to an operator. It was way cool.

What a comfort knowing that as he journeys across country even on the loneliest of roads, he is never alone if he needs help. There is a higher power available to him. As we journey through life, we need to know we are not alone. There is a higher power that is available to us. So many times we think we have to do it all ourselves. A faith-based belief system is a great thing. I personally have a belief and relationship with God the creator of the universe through Jesus Christ. You may or may not share that same belief system. That is okay. This isn't about church, it is about you. It is about your vision, dreams and goals.

I want to help you see how a relationship with a higher power can be a key in PowerAchieving. I have some, perhaps unconventional views on how this is all tied together. I would ask that you open your mind and explore with me. This segment is not designed to convert you to anything except achieving all that you deserve in this life. Fair enough?

In this journey of life, there are most definitely going to be highs and lows, good times and bad times. There will be joy and there will be pain. There are going to be times that we laugh and times that we cry. Having a higher power to share these times with takes the pressure off of us. This isn't about being perfect. This is about the times when you are down and feel all alone. Having someone to share your burden, having a relationship with God helps when you take time to meditate on him and whisper a soft prayer of help or thanks. I am not saying that you have to look or act a certain way or change your style of anything. If that happens, cool. If it doesn't, okay. A relationship with the creator, your higher power, God, is a very personal thing and should be between you and God, period.

The "Higher Power" concept is not about putting on a spiritual show for anyone. It is about you having a rock to hold on to when the seas of life get rough. This life can get rough. This life can get confusing. We all need to have a faith that we can hold on to when those times come. But not just in times of need. We really start PowerAchieving when we develop that higher power relationship in the good times. When things are good, we need to take a little time from our morning or at the end of the day and quiet ourselves and offer up a prayer of thanks.

There are many studies that are coming out that promote the health benefits of prayer. I believe that the mind, the body and the spirit are all connected. It is hard to achieve without all three components. It is like driving a car on only three tires. Your ride is smoother on all four. Your life is smoother when you include the "Higher Power". Don't neglect your spiritual needs. A higher power is just that—POWER.

Communicating with the "Higher Power" is a two-way street. It is not only good to share your thoughts and heart by offering a daily prayer, but I have to tell you, there are some awesome nuggets of life in the bible. Little treasures of life. I would suggest getting a little devotional book. Make a habit of reading something inspirational or positive each morning and again before you go to bed. There are hundreds of great little devotion and inspirational books. Many are available on my website, www.powerachievers.com.

Take the time to tap into your personal, private, spiritual dimension. If you are going to achieve your goals and make your visions and dreams a reality, you need to understand and use the "Higher Power" to give you peace in your life. I explain it like this. If your car quit running, you would call a mechanic. If your pipes were leaking, you would call a plumber. If your life needs some repair, why not call on the creator of life? The "Higher Power" will be one of the most important powers as you PowerAchieve.

As We Journey Through Life, We Need To Know That We Are Not Alone

"Power" Page

List ways that you can draw upon your spiritual strength.

8
The "Power of the Choice"

What was the first thing you did when you woke up this morning? When your alarm clock went off, whether it is one of those clocks that wake you up to music, or rings, or maybe someone whispered "time to get up" into your ear, what was the first thing you did? I asked this of someone at a seminar once and they said, "Opened my eyes". That is the process of waking up, not an action after you woke up. Some of you reached over and hit the snooze button. Some got up and went to the bathroom. Some rolled over and kissed their mate. But in reality, those are not really the first things you did. Those are the first movements you made. You first made a choice. You made a choice to make those movements. You chose to hit the snooze. You chose to go to the bathroom. For some that was a good choice. The first thing we do in the morning is make a conscious choice. And that is really all that we are going to do the rest of that day.

We make choices about what to wear, what size coffee we are going to get on the way to the office, who we are going to talk too, what time we are going to meet. Think about it. Your entire day is spent making choices. You make a conscious choice about every fifteen seconds. When you break it down, life is really nothing more than a series of choices. You make good ones and good things can happen. You make bad ones and bad things can happen. That sounds simple.

It sounds simple because it is simple. We make life too complex sometimes.

There is tremendous power in the choice. One of the greatest gifts that the good Lord gave us is the power to choose. It is easy to take this awesome gift for granted. Once you understand the "Power of the Choice", you can understand that you have the power to live the life that you envision and have always dreamed of. It can be yours. You can choose to achieve all that you have desired. You can choose to make your vision a reality and succeed in life.

Your Choices Will Determine Your Achievement

Choices are in many ways like cells. Millions and millions of cells make up our bodies. Millions and millions of choices make up our life. Choices seem like such small things, but one choice leads to another choice and another, and another until we have a history. We can look back at the choices we have made and we will see our life in retrospect. We can go back into our memory and review our life. Our memory plays back our life like a movie and we see the choices we have made and how our life has been affected by those choices. We can literally, physically, see our past. Each choice you make today will become a permanent part of your life. Understanding the "Power of the Choice" will help you see your future. Our memory plays back our past like a movie and our vision shows us the coming attractions. You can write the script through your choices.

When your life is done, you will have left a painting of your life for others to see. Each choice is like a brush stroke on the canvas of your life. You see a painted picture in your mind of your life. You see where you have been; you visualize where you want to go. You are currently standing in the dimension of time called "now". You have the paintbrush of choice in your hand. The choices you make today will paint your future, which will ultimately become your past. *Make your life a masterpiece.*

Choices that we make today affect the future. As a sophomore in high school, I was a four foot eleven inch, 98 pound lost kid. I was not big enough to be a jock. Not smart enough to be in the honor society. Not rich enough to be a prep. I was just a typical struggling 16 year old. In April 1974, my sophomore year, a tornado ripped through my hometown. It was one of America's worst natural disasters. The 2 mile wide twister engulfed the little town of 25,000. I remember standing in the front yard with my sister and dad. I saw whole houses being picked up and being sucked into this great funnel as if they were made of something less than cardboard. My dad, in a panic, put his kids in the car and drove away from the ever-growing mass of wind. As we came back into town from the backside of the monster cloud, people were still getting up off the ground. Eighteen wheel tractor-trailers and trucks were on top of three-story buildings. A train blown off the tracks blocked the main street of the town. Buildings that had stood for centuries were gone without a trace. It goes without saying that the schools, all of them, were blown away. There would be no more school, or so we thought.

We thought it was cool until they made us go to school from 4 pm until 9 pm at a neighboring county. I had signed up to go to vocational school as a junior to study carpentry. Mind you, I had flunked wood shop but I wanted to build your house. The next school year, the city managed to fix one school building up and were going to run split sessions for junior and senior high. The high school went from 7:20 am until 12:00 noon. The vocational school that I had signed up for went from 7:30 am until 2:30 pm. I was short and skinny, not dumb. I switched back from vocational school to high school so I could get out 2 hours early. I took courses I had never heard of. I took courses like public speaking and drama. To everyone's amazement, I excelled at both and ended up majoring in theatre in college. I make my living doing public speaking. That one single, solitary choice to change back from vocational school, for whatever reason, changed the course and direction of my life forever.

There Is Tremendous Power In Your Choices

The power to choose can work for the positive or the negative. Our choices will have an effect on our lives. Along with the power to choose, we must understand that there is a responsibility that goes with each choice. If you choose to hit the snooze alarm in the morning, you are going to be faced with a laundry list of other choices. "If I sleep an extra 15 minutes, do I wash my hair? Do I sneak in the back door so the boss does not see me? Do I drive a little faster to work? What if I get a ticket?" Choices we make cause powerful actions that are never ending. Choices cause a ripple effect. Mastering the "Power of the Choice" is an absolute key to making our way through life and making our vision a reality.

Not every choice is easy or pleasant. In your life, or in your career, you have undoubtedly been faced with having to make a difficult and uncomfortable choice. We anguish over such tough choices trying to reach a decision. It seems there is so much riding on this one choice and maybe there is. A break up of a relationship, a career move, a major financial move. All are very big choices of what to do. Big choices typically are led up to by a series of other choices until it leads to the "pivot point" choice.

When you reach the pivot point choice, you know that when you make this choice there will be significant change take place. This is usually the time when we understand just exactly how powerful the choice can be. When you reach the pivot point, the change is usually great and the responsibility large. An example of a pivot point choice would be choosing to get married or quitting your job. Both of these choices will cause great change. The big choices are not the only choices that carry power. All choices have power. The great thing about that power is that you are in control of that power.

The power to choose is yours. The responsibility that comes with those choices is also yours. I speak to many groups and like to tell the story of the Indian Brave who is faced with a choice. Legend has it that when you are fourteen years old, that is the time you must prove your manhood to the others in the tribe. At fourteen the Indian Brave walks out of his tepee and is looking for a task that will prove his manhood. He looks up and sees this huge mountain. "That's it. I will climb the mountain to prove my manhood." He goes back into the tepee and puts his buckskin jacket on because he knows it is going to be cold. He can see the snow on top of the mountain. He takes off to climb the mountain and after hours of climbing, the Indian Brave makes it to the top. His hands are bruised, his clothes are dirty, but he has climbed the mountain. The air is crisp and clear. The snow crunches under his feet. He can see for miles. It is beautiful. He looks down and he sees a snake. The snake looks up at him and says, "Get mmmeee down from hheere...I'mmmm freezing." The Brave looked down and said, "No, you are a snake and if I pick you up, you will bite me." "No, I won't," insisted the snake. "If I stay up here, I will die...just get me down." The boy thought for a minute, "No, you are a snake. If I pick you up you will bite me." "No, I won't. I swear...just get me down," the snake begged. The Brave reluctantly picked the snake up and put it inside of his buckskin jacket to keep it warm. They got down to the bottom of the mountain. The boy took the snake out of his jacket and threw it on the ground to set it free just like it had asked. The snake turned around, coiled up and bit him. The boy grabbed his leg and felt the blood. His blood. He said to the snake, "You promised...you swore to me that you would not bite me! You gave me your word." The snake said, "Hey, you knew what I was all of the time…you should never have picked me up."

The Power To Choose Is Yours, But So Is The Responsibility

When you make a choice, you then become the owner of the consequences and responsibilities that go along with that choice. Choose carefully. If you still haven't seen just how much power you have when you understand the "Power of the Choice", consider how these choices have affected us and changed our world forever. Choices from people just like you and me. Their choices have had an extraordinary impact on our world as we know it. Abraham Lincoln chose to go against the grain and popular opinion to abolish slavery. Harry Truman chose to drop the atomic bomb on Hiroshima. Sam Phillips from Sun Records chose to record a skinny kid named Elvis. These choices, had they not been made or had they been made differently, would have changed the landscape of this great country. There is awesome power in the gift that the Lord has given us…the power to choose.

"Power" Page

List some choices that will help you
achieve more in your career and personal life.

9
The "Power of Action"

The choice is powerful, but not by itself. A choice is like a stick of dynamite. The dynamite is powerful but it only works when the fuse is lit. You can choose to lose weight or you can choose to make more money or whatever your vision is. Choosing is only part of the equation. Just as the stick of dynamite is powerful, the power is only released when the fuse is lit. When it comes to your choices you must light the fuse of action to make it work. Just as faith without works is dead, a choice without action is just a good intention.

I was talking to a friend of mine one day and she began talking about how she really needed to lose weight and by golly, she was going to start eating better and go to the gym and get in shape. She was as sincere as anyone I have ever heard. She had it planned out. Then as God is my witness, she ordered a banana split. I was so mad. What happened? She chose to work out, she chose to eat right...in her mind, but she didn't have the action to make the choice that she had made, into a reality. You can choose to join a gym but if you never go after you join, what does it matter? Her choice became nothing more than good intentions because there was no action. Faith without works is dead.

Imagine for a moment that you are on a movie set in Hollywood. Julia Roberts is in this film. There are lots of people that are buzzing around. The crew sets up the shot.

The makeup artist puts powder on the actors' faces. The director discusses the scene with Julia and her co-star, Tom Cruise. This is pretty exciting. The actors have their lines and everybody takes their places. The director yells, "Quiet on the set," and everyone stands still. Nothing happens until the director yells, "Action!" Nothing happens in life until you take action. Can I say one thing to you...ACTION! You have made choices for your life and only when you take action will those choices become manifested into real life.

A Choice Without Action Is Just A Good Intention

What is keeping you from taking action on some of the choices you have made for your life? Do you put off even making choices because you know that you will have to take action? I know so many people who are afraid of success. They are not afraid of failing. They have failing down to a science. They are afraid of succeeding. Failing is easy; you don't have to do much to fail. No hard choices to make, no action to take and no accountability if you try and don't make it. Action takes effort, failing does not take effort. You can do nothing and fail. Some people are fully confident in their ability to fail. It is their ability to succeed that has their confidence shaken. Success is waiting on you to take action.

Some people don't believe they can do it, so they make the choice to do something but they don't back it up with action. Then they use the comforting thought that choosing was a good enough try. Part of them says, "Well we tried," and the other part of them says, "yeah, but not very hard."

Getting yourself to take action is like the cartoons. Remember the cartoons where there is a demon on one shoulder and an angel on another. The demon is saying one thing and the angel is saying another. This happens to all of us when we make a difficult conscious choice. The demon of doubt is on one shoulder saying, "You can't do that...remember that one time in kindergarten when you wet your pants...you are no good, you could never achieve that." The angel of action is on the other shoulder saying, "Don't listen to him...you are smart...you can do this. Go ahead, make it happen...you can." You think to yourself, "Yes, I can." The demon of doubt says, "Yeah right, you got fired from that one job remember? You will never work out." The angel of action says, "That was a long time ago...you can do anything." And the struggle goes on and on and on. Please understand that THE DEMON OF DOUBT PLAYS ON OUR PAST FAILURES. If we added up all of the dumb stuff we have done in our lives, we probably would go crawl in a hole and never come out. *Don't let your past make you afraid of your future.* Live in the now. Seize the "Power of the Choice".

The real "Power of the Choice" is not just in choosing, but then lighting the fuse of action. Choices will have a cause and effect that will produce change. We need to know how to handle change. Many people come to a point in life where they discover that they need to make some serious choices about their life. Maybe you are there right now. You are in a place in life where you are thinking to yourself, "This isn't how I wanted things to turn out." My vision and my reality are two separate things. People faced with making changes need to look at the long term effect of those changes. Life changes need to be thought out so that they are lasting changes.

Life is not a unicycle. It just doesn't turn around or spin around on a dime. Life is more like an airplane. If you are flying along, cruising at 30,000 feet, smooth, and then all of the sudden the plane drops, then takes a sharp turn to the left, you will take notice. I don't know about you, but when this happens, I am looking for a way out. This happened to me on a flight from Bozeman, Montana. I had been doing training sessions for a large corporation in Charlotte, North Carolina for about a month. After the training was done, I decided that I would go from Charlotte to Bozeman to visit my friends, Phil and Kara. I had never been to Montana. It was beautiful! The scenery was breathtaking. I had a great time. On the flight back I was sleeping on the plane when I heard the seatbelt indicator ding. I made sure my seatbelt was secure. I just started to doze back off when the plane hit an air pocket. We dropped about 700 feet in about 5 seconds. I just about came unglued! My heart was in my throat. My palms were sweating and my heart was pounding. I was scared. I am thinking, "Abort" because I know this is not normal.

The airplane, because of outside influences such as turbulence and air thermals, got out of control for a minute. Our life can sometimes seem out of control from outside influences. The direction and course of the airplane was changed in an instant. The instant change was unnatural and caused the passengers to become unnerved. Instant change is almost always unnatural. The pilot corrected the course of the airplane by performing a number of tasks in a systematic order to bring the airplane back under control. It only took the airplane about five seconds to drop out of control. It took the pilot about thirty seconds to get back on course. In order to get back on course, you may need to make changes that will be systematic and take time. Sometimes slow, steady changes are the most important ones. Getting out of control can sometimes happen in an instant, but getting back under control may take longer than we think. Be patient.

An airplane changes its course with small adjustments from the tail rudder and wings. The tail rudder and wings move only 4" to 8" when the pilot controls them. Very small adjustments make a huge difference. Slight changes can turn a 50-ton jet a completely different direction. Slight adjustments and changes can turn your life into a new direction. You may not need to make drastic changes. You may need to make slight adjustments. You are the pilot of your plane. Are you on course? Do you need to change your flight plan?

Choices Will Have A Cause And Effect That Will Produce Change

I work with many people in the sales profession on building sales skills. Selling is a craft. The sales professional is like an artist. The truly good and successful sales professionals understand the process that is involved in their craft and how slight changes in work habit or presentation can make the difference between making the sale and losing the sale. I had a business acquaintance that sold supplemental insurance to cover a client if they ever found themselves in a nursing home or an extended care facility. Pat Finch was an honest hard working woman who was well respected in our community. Pat called me one day and explained that she was having a terrible time closing sales and asked if I would consider coaching her. We set up a session and the first thing I did was have Pat show me the presentation in a role-playing situation. I said, "I'll play the client and you sell me." Pat went through all of the introductory business and then got into her presentation. I, as the prospect, listened with an open mind. Pat's presentation was just like they taught her—canned. As she went through the "benefits" of the plan I stopped her. I said, "Lets reverse roles."

I did the same presentation using her presentation book. I made one small change. I picked up the pace by about half. Not too fast but fast enough to keep the interest and the prospect thinking. I then got to the close and I created my own close. I said, "Mrs. Prospect, I don't want to be nosy but how long have you worked?" "About forty years," Pat answered playing the part. "And can you give me…in round numbers, how much you have managed to save over those forty years?" I continued. "Well,"…Pat hesitated. "Just a ballpark figure," I said with an wisp of casualness. "About forty thousand dollars I guess," Pat said. "That's great," I said with a touch of pride. "I bet you were a hard worker too. The kind of employee the company needed. Was it hard to save money while raising a family?" I asked. My voice now had the inflection that took her back to those days. I was painting a word picture for her. As soon as she nodded her head "yes" I leaned into her with my body language as if I was telling her a secret, and said, "Forty thousand dollars is a lot of money, but do you realize that in today's economy if you got sick and had to have extended care, forty thousand dollars would last only about five months?" I paused to let that sink in for a second. I lowered my voice a bit and leaned in just a bit more and then continued, "Wouldn't it make sense to pay twenty dollars a month and let XYZ Insurance Company take all of the risk and you keep your forty thousand that you worked so hard to save?" Pat looked at me like the light bulb had just gone on. She paused for a second and said, "Wow, that's good!"

I didn't make big changes to her presentation. I just made little adjustments. I made changes where they needed to be made. Guess who was the next month's sales leader? That's right, Pat Finch. Small adjustments took Pat from the bottom of the sales team to the top. Make small changes first.

So many times we decide to make changes and we start implementing those changes and we get out of our normal comfort zone. People choose to make changes and they get all fired up and motivated to make those changes; "I am going to lose weight and get in shape. I am going to get a new job. I am going to change this or that." Sometimes the changes are too many all at once. Just like the airplane, when we make too many changes all at once, we feel out of control. We get nervous, fear sets in, then doubt, and then we abort the journey because we are out of our comfort level. We go back to where we were, back to home base; the changes were too many too fast. Make changes in your life that will start out small and then grow. It is very hard to turn your life around on a dime. Slow, steady changes will last.

If you choose to lose weight, don't jump in and try to run five miles; do two aerobic tapes and lift weights all in the same day. Start slow and steady, as you feel comfortable. A basic law of life is really contrary to how we think in this instant world we live in. We are so used to wanting and getting everything now. Nuke it for two minutes, add milk and stir are formulas we use in today's world. These formulas are good for warming up leftovers or making chocolate milk, but not for managing change in our lives. A building is built one brick or block at a time. Roads are constructed one mile at a time. Marathons are run one step at a time. Changes in your life need to be managed one choice at a time.

You can choose the changes for your life all at one time, but you may not want to take action on those choices all at the same time. You should put the choices of change in order. You should make a plan and then manage that plan. Don't be afraid to light the fuse of action that will ignite the "Power of the Choice" and cause an explosion of positive change in your life. A person walks through life painting a portrait not of what they should have done or would have done or even could have done. They paint a portrait of what they did. The greatest mistake you can make in life is to be continually fearing that you will make one. Most people spend their life planning the future and regretting the past. Don't leave this life with regrets. Leave this life having lived your dreams and having made your vision a reality.

Make A Plan And Then Manage That Plan

"Power" Page

List some small changes that you need to make
that will turn your life around and put you on course.

10
The "Power of Now"

The time is now. Don't ever forget that. A common mistake that people make and a key reason people don't achieve is that they don't live in the now. People forget to live in the now. There is power in the now. Now is where you are. For better or worse, "the now" is the dimension of time that you live in. It is where you are. This moment in time is all that we are given. In the twinkling of an eye your time could be up. Yesterday is history. Tomorrow is the future. Today is a gift, that is why it is called the "present." Because we live in the now does not mean that we discount the future. I for one am very interested in the future; that is where I am going to spend the rest of my life.

Planning your future is kind of like taking a vacation by car across this great country. Traveling with my family was a trip (pun intended). As a kid, we often took family vacations to Florida by car. What great family bonding experiences those trips were. My dad was the consummate traveler. He would have to go from point A to point B in better time than he made it last year. My sister and I would be in the back seat. We would be bored so we would invent little games. Games like roll the window down, roll the window up. Roll the window down, roll the window up. Then, we would start racing, rolling the window down, rolling the window up.

My mom hated this game. She would be in the front seat, "Stop that...stop that...I said stop that." So we would "stop that" and then we would start fighting. All of a sudden dad had had enough of this and looks in the rear view mirror with the death glare and says, "Boy, do you want me to stop this car and wear you out?" I always wanted to say, "Yeah, pull this bad boy over." Ah, that may have been a bad choice.

My sister was the smart one on those trips. By the time we got from Ohio to Florida, she had somehow gotten all of this money. She had acquired all kinds of change and dollar bills. She had loads of it. I asked my mom how Connie gets all of this money, which was news to my mom. After investigating, it seems my sister was "finding" this money on the table after we would eat at a restaurant. My sister was scooping up the tips my dad left. We never stopped at Stuckey's again.

Imagine if you will, you are on vacation and you stop the first day. You want to see the sights, maybe go to the pool, but you had to stay in the room so you could plan the next day's activities. Then when you get to the next day, you spend more time planning what you are going to see two days later. You don't get to do the things you planned yesterday because you are busy planning tomorrow. Most of the time is spent planning and a little time vacationing. Then when the trip is over, you are exhausted because you spent all of your time planning and stressing about what to do rather than enjoying the moment. Plan the future but live in the now.

Today Is A Gift, That Is Why It Is Called The "Present"

Understanding the "Power of Now" is really simple. Think with me here. You can only execute your plan while in the now, today. You can plan the future, but you have to wait until the future becomes today before you can take action and make the plan a reality. The "Power of Now" is the fact that all of your planning is brought to fruition when the plan is worked or executed, and that only happens in the now. Until then, it is only a plan and when the moment passes, it becomes history. The now is powerful. What you do today, right now, is important. Time is a funny thing. It stops for no man. It is our most precious commodity. The future is coming whether you are ready or not.

We tend to look at the big picture when we think of time. We think of weeks, months and years. We don't think of now or today. What is today? Name some significant events that have happened in your life. The *day* you were born, your first *day* of school, graduation *day*, the *day* you turned 18, your wedding *day*, your first *day* on the job. The point is, our life is benchmarked by important DAYS in our life. You need to understand the power of today, the now. What can you do with today? Today you can take action on a choice you have made. Today you can start that exercise program you have been thinking about. Today you can meet new people. Today you can mend fences from the past. Today you can start eating healthy. Today you can start the rest of your life. You can do it NOW.

Yesterday Is A Cancelled Check, Tomorrow Is A Promissory Note, Today Is Cash
Spend It Wisely

This has been an exciting segment to me—The "Power of the Choice", the "Power of Action", and the "Power of Now". Choice, Action, Now. C.A.N., as in "You CAN." You "CAN" achieve your dreams when you understand and implement these powers into your life. Think of the choices that you want to make that will be positive changes for you. Go to the Power Page at the back of this chapter and list 10 choices that will change your life, and then narrow it down to the five most important. Write the choice down at the top of the page. Under the choice, write down the things that need to happen to make that change happen. Write down the action that needs to take place. Now under that, write down a timeframe to achieve the change. You are helping the five choices become real. Take action towards the goal each day. Execute in the now. You will be amazed at how you make your vision a reality after you clarify your choice, start the action, and make the now your ally. Build on it each day until you have turned "*potential*" into "*reality*."

Choose To Take Action Now

"Power" Page

List the choices that demand action and
list what action is needed.

11
The "Power of Time"

Time waits for no man. The tiny grains of sand run through the hourglass of our lives. Each one seemingly faster than the last. Time is perhaps the one power that we cannot control. We can however, manage the "Power of Time". Think about it; what is your life? It is a vapor that appears for just a little while and then vanishes. It is a flower, which blooms and then fades away. The clock is ticking.

George Burns once said, "If you want to make your dreams come true, don't fall in love with your bed." The "Power of Time" demands our respect. Each person on this earth is given the exact same amount of time each day, 24 hours, 1,440 minutes a day, 86,400 seconds. That is all. We cannot go into the past and get any of those minutes back. They are gone forever. Those minutes, like the grains of sand in the hourglass, pass through and cannot be retrieved. Our life is too short and time is too important to spend moments of our life hating, fearing and living in anger. We must respect the time that the good Lord has given us. You must respect the opportunity that is in front of you to achieve your vision, dreams and goals. Respect the gift of time and turn that gift into something powerful.

I believe that there is a time for everything. A time to work, a time to rest, a time to give, a time to take. I just don't believe that all of those times are equal. If you spend as much time resting as you do working, it will take you twice as long to achieve your goal. In the world of auto racing, each second is critical. In the Daytona 500 stock car race, cars move at 100 yards each second. That is over 200 mph! When a racer such as four-time NASCAR champ, Jeff Gordon, brings his race car into the pits for new tires and gas, the stop lasts only about 15 seconds. That is an amazing feat for the crew. They change four tires and fill the car with gas in 15 seconds. Each second that they are in the pits will cost them time on the race track. If Jeff Gordon took a break and got out of his car and stretched his legs, stood around talked to his crew, signed a few autographs, all of the other cars in the race would pass him up 2-3 times. You can only be a champion when you learn how to manage the "Power of Time". There is a time to take a break, but that time is not in the middle of the race. Do you spend more time resting or racing to your goal?

I find that many people don't respect the "Power of Time". Most people think that they have plenty of it; therefore, they put off today's tasks until tomorrow. Their future calendar is packed with "gonna do's" but their schedule today is "open". Putting today's tasks on tomorrow's calendar is not time management.

PowerAchieving is designed to help you achieve— today. Understanding and managing the "Power of Time" is a crucial element. We must understand that time is moving. The life meter is running, just like a taxicabs meter runs in New York City. We can't afford to waste time. Killing time is suicide. Tomorrow is a promissory note, yesterday is a cancelled check, today is cash. Spend it wisely.

I believe there are three keys to managing the "Power of Time". The number one key in managing the "Power of Time" is to prioritize. Every day you are faced with many tasks to complete. Some of those tasks are more important than others. Achieving more in the 1,440 minutes you have been given each day will depend upon you sorting out the more important tasks from the less important. What makes one task more important than another could differ. Maybe something needs to be completed by a time deadline. Maybe the financial reward is greater for one task more than another. You must decide the order of importance.

I used to work with a guy who got fired from the company because he had his priorities out of whack. He was the ultimate disrespector of the "Power of Time". Every Friday he would leave the office mid-morning and go pay his bills. That's right, he would go to each store or creditor and pay his bills in person. I guess he never heard of the post office. While he was out, he would stop for lunch, go by his house to check the mail and messages. Was it that important to hand deliver his bills and stop by his house? How high was that on the priority list? Paying bills are important, but the effort of hand delivering them was not a priority. He would mismanage 4-5 hours a week by misprioritizing. It is not like he over achieved the rest of the week. This co-worker was the kind of guy who would be in a meeting and have to leave to take a call and never come back to the meeting. When he did this, I would go to his office only to find him playing a computer game. I talked to him a few weeks ago and he was filling me in on what was new. He said he was working on a book. When I mentioned that he was working on one a couple of years ago he said it was the same one but he is closer to getting it done. I think he spends more time resting than racing. He mismanaged four hours a week just by not prioritizing his tasks. Do the math. Four hours a week multiplied by four weeks multiplied by 12 months is 11,520 minutes a year. 11,500 minutes of mismanagement. That is 8 days. He lost over an entire week of time. It was time that he lost and could not get back. The sad part was that he had nothing to show for it.

Putting Today's Tasks On Tomorrow's Calender Is Not Time Management

If you are going to take advantage of the "Power of Time", I believe that you should stop and analyze your strengths and your weaknesses as they apply to how you manage the time that you are given. Analyze your strengths in time management. We are all given the same amount of time in each day; however, how we use that time could separate the dreamers from those who are "living" their dreams. Think about how waking up just 20 minutes early could dramatically change your life. That is 2.5 hours each week that you can use to reach your goal and make your vision a reality.

Think about the positive power of giving yourself an extra 20 minutes each day. By getting out of bed an extra 20 minutes each day, you add an incredible 130 hours to your ability to achieve this year. By adding 20 minutes of time to each day, you actually add over three, forty-hour work weeks to your year. You must use this time to work on achieving. Is it worth getting out of bed 20 minutes early to live your dreams and make your vision a reality? If you can implement this strategy, which I call "20 Minutes to Achievement", this would be a great strength. As strange as it sounds, getting out of bed early and adding an extra 20 minutes a day and working could be the difference between just "having" a dream and "living" your dream.

20 Minutes To Achievement—Do It

The old saying, "Work hard and play hard" is a lifestyle choice for me. The pitfall in that philosophy however, is if you become unbalanced. You can't take a week off and play hard, vacation, relax, travel or whatever and then come back and take two weeks to "get back into the swing". The same energy level that you have on vacation or playing must be used when you get back to work. The key for this of course, is to prioritize, organize and execute. Do you know people that come back from vacation and on the first day back, spend the first two hours telling everyone who has an ear about their trip? Then they say, "I have a zillion messages, I just don't know where to start." And because they don't know where to start, they don't. If you don't start, you can't finish. If you don't finish, you can't achieve. When attacking the tasks that are before you, you must start by creating a plan. Prioritize the tasks. Write them down on a sheet of paper and then number them in order of importance. Work from this list and this list only. Do you prioritize? Is prioritizing a strength or weakness? Make it a strength.

The Key To A Successful Organization Is Organization

THE POWER OF ORGANIZATION:
Once you have your priorities in line, you must organize. I designed a line of motivational posters. One of the posters is "The Ten Commandments of Business Success". Commandment number 4 is "The key to a successful organization is organization." Looking at your list of priorities, take the first and then organize the plan of attack. For example, I have to put a presentation together for a group of investors for a project. The priority has moved from warm to hot. It has moved from the back burner to the front burner. It was moved from the back burner to the front because of a deadline. As the meeting time draws near and other priorities are completed, this one moves up. I must be organized because this presentation is potentially worth between one and five million dollars. I need to break down all of the little tasks involved in this presentation. Those tasks are written down on a "hit list", or some people call them "to do" lists. The hit list reads something like this:

1) Secure meeting space in conference room
2) Order light snacks and drinks for meeting
3) Research subject matter
4) Research source and download photos of project
5) Develop PowerPoint presentation
6) Create proforma for potential investors

You must be organized and get the priorities completed in a systematic manner.

THE POWER OF EXECUTION:

Like a great sculptor chips away at a huge block of stone until he or she has a work of art completed, you must chip away at each task until you have the project finished. When a sculptor looks upon a block of stone, they have a vision of what they want to create. You also have a vision. The sculptor must prioritize. The sculptor must decide where to start. The sculptor must choose where to chip away and in what order. Do they start at the top, bottom, or at the side of the stone? There are priorities. The sculptor has a plan. The sculptor is organized. They have the right tools and know when each chip must be made. Having prioritized and being organized is of little value if the sculptor doesn't pick up the hammer and start EXECUTING the plan. In managing the "Power of Time", you too must start chipping away at your tasks. Execute the plan.

A) Prioritize
B) Organize
C) Execute

Execution is the payoff and the result of managing the "Power of Time". Managing the "Power of Time" is a lot like target practice with a gun. My dad belonged to a gun club when I was growing up. I used to tag along and watch as he competed against other shooters. The shooters took three basic steps to complete their round. Ready-Aim-Fire. The shooters would prioritize by choosing the most valuable or highest point targets. They were organized. There was a calm systematic method to shooting each target in the correct order. The most important action was actually pulling the trigger. You can have your priorities in order, you can be organized and know exactly what you are going to do, but until you execute, until you pull the trigger, you will never hit your target. In short, managing the time that you have been given and making that time into something powerful is really about completing each task.

I have a business style that can be summed up as, "see the deal—do the deal". That style doesn't have to be just about business. That style can be applied to lots of areas of our life. See your vision, prioritize, organize and execute the plan. When you do that, your vision will become reality and you have turned time into a powerful tool instead of something that slips away from you. You can manage the "Power of Time". When you learn how to use the "Power of Time" to help you achieve, you will complete small tasks. Completing small tasks are steps on your journey to achievement. Each journey starts with the first step followed by hundreds of other small steps. When you take single steps, one after the other, the next thing you know, you will have walked miles. Prioritizing, organizing and executing will keep you from walking those miles in a circle. Move straight ahead. Move toward your goals. Your vision is in front of you; walk straight to it. Make your vision a reality. Don't just dream; live your dreams. Why? Because it is time.

"Power" Page

List ways that you could better use the time that
you have been given as a gift from the creator.

12
The "Power of Giving"

I contend that there are two kinds of people in this world. There are givers and takers. We all do both at some time, but our predominant trait is either one or the other. We are either a giver or taker. Most people on the surface see the taker as the powerful one. I call people who see things this way mentally dyslexic. They have it BACKWARDS. Actually, the power is in giving. It sounds strange, but it is true. Giving is a natural power position.

When an animal trainer trains an animal such as a bear or a dog to do commands, the reward is typically giving the animal food or treats. Who has the power in this case? The giver. Why? Because the animal wants the treat so much it will do what it takes to get it. Do you go to work for free? No, you go because they "give" you a paycheck. If you wanted a raise from your boss, who would have the power? Your boss has the power. Your boss can say "yes" or "no". The boss is the giver of the raise. The boss has the power. If that is not true, then why are you nervous about asking for a raise?

There was a bear that was used in movies named Bart. Bart was a Hollywood star. Bart learned to perform for the cameras by being rewarded with blueberries and salmon. He was given food. He knew if he wanted to get a piece of salmon, he would have to perform. People's behavior changes when they are given a gift such as tickets to a game or the theatre.

People will go the extra mile for you when you give to them. Bart the bear died May 10th, 2000. Doug and Lynne Seus were Bart's owners. They received Bart from a U.S. zoo and gave him an incredible life of performing, but most importantly, Bart was able to live in a natural habitat. Doug and Lynne founded an organization called "Vital Ground" which allows bears and all kinds of wild animals to live in their natural environment.

Bart starred in many movies including "The Gambler", and his brother, Bear Tank, is also a star with movie credits that include "Dr. DooLittle" with Eddie Murphy. Doug and Lynne Seus have, through their foundation, Vital Ground, bought thousands of acres of land in key western states to give the animals a home that is as natural and untouched by man as it was hundreds of years ago. Without Doug and Lynne giving back, these awesome creatures may have been snuffed out. Who has the power to preserve this wonderful animal? The givers, Doug and Lynne Seus.

There is a world of truth in the phrase, "it is better to give than receive." Unfortunately, I find that takers out number givers four to one. There are more people willing to take than to give. These are the people who never offer to buy lunch even though you bought the last three times. These are the people who cut you off in the parking lot to get that parking spot. Takers never seem to ask you about your life. They would rather tell you about theirs. Taking is easy, there is no sacrifice involved. Giving is hard. It involves sacrifice, confidence, faith and most of all, heart.

I am not talking about giving just to get something. I am talking about giving out of the goodness of your heart. Faith comes into play when we give and don't expect anything in return. It is hard knowing that when you give something, you probably won't receive anything in return. Most of the time you don't receive even a thank you. A person who gives because they want to meet a need or show kindness must be secure and confident in themselves because they won't receive immediate material gratification. The gratification comes from within.

Givers Are Stronger Than Takers

There are people who give only to get. I call them investment givers. These are the people who give for the sole purpose of getting back more than they gave. You will notice investment givers at cocktail parties or social functions. These are the people who hand out a compliment by saying, "Oh your dress is fabulous," and then stand there with the "Okay, say something nice about me" look on their face. They are not true givers and are missing the "Power of Giving" altogether. The "Power of Giving" only works when it comes from the heart and doesn't expect a return on investment.

A giver will be confident, have faith, and make sacrifices. A giver is also something else, vulnerable. No matter how much a person is a giver, sometimes it is nice to receive. A giver's heart is less guarded. When a giver gives and gives and doesn't get anything back, a giver shuts down for a period of time to recharge. That is when people usually ask, "What is wrong with you?" Sometimes it hurts to give. A marriage or relationship can suffer when there is one who is the taker and one who is the giver. When they say a relationship is give and take, they don't mean one of each. Because opposites attract, typically there is a giver and a taker in a relationship. The relationship is strained when the giver gives until there is no more to give emotionally. In order to live in harmony, each person must give.

The "Power of Giving" is simply this. If you had a room full of takers, after a period of time, there would be nothing left. It would all be taken. But, if you have a room full of givers, there will always be plenty because givers are giving to each other. Think of our economy. The economy of our country is not built on cash. It is built and only works when cash is flowing. The economy only works when there is an exchange of money through commerce. When people stop buying things, the economy shuts down. Without givers, our world would shut down.

This week I experienced a wonderful example of how the "Power of Giving" works. I have season tickets to the University of Dayton Flyer basketball games. On the way to the radio station to do my weekly radio show, I stopped at the Dairy Mart for a cup of coffee. The Flyers had a basketball game that afternoon. If I was going to go, I would have to rush off the air and hurry to the arena to keep from missing the game. I was talking to the manager of the Dairy Mart and found out that he liked basketball. I gave him my tickets so he could take his son. When I got to the radio station, I told my producer, Jim, that I gave my tickets away but I still really wanted to go. He said, "You're in luck, I have an extra ticket from the station that you can have." I took the ticket and met Jim at the arena. We ended up sitting with a client of mine in prime seats. Everyone won; the manager at Dairy Mart got to take his son to the game, I got to go, and Jim got to meet people and sit courtside. All because people gave.

How can you use the "Power of Giving" to help you achieve your vision, desires and goals? Give without reservation. Don't expect something in return. The good book says, "freely you have received, freely give." In the business world it is amazing how many people want to do business with givers. Don't give to get, and there is that temptation. Give because you can.

Years ago I had a friend who worked as a manager of a local restaurant. Kenny and Jackie had a small son 6 years old. Kenny didn't make much money and on top of that, he had been burned in an accident at the restaurant and was off work. He was only drawing a Worker's Compensation check. I knew they were really struggling so I really felt impressed to help. I saw their car at the grocery store. It was a summer night and the windows were down in his car. I had just cashed my payroll check, so I pulled up and put the entire $700 on his front seat. I pulled across the parking lot to watch. I wanted to make sure nobody stole it. You know how those "takers" can be. I saw Kenny and Jackie come out and get into the car.

After they drove off, I went home. I had been home awhile when the phone rang. Kenny called and told me that someone left $700 on his seat. He said no one could have known they needed almost $700 for rent and a car repair. I really didn't know that. That was just what my check was that week. I said to Kenny, "Wow, that is cool, the good Lord was looking out for you." I never told anyone this story until now. Did I get anything out of it? Nope. Doesn't matter. I didn't give to get, I gave because I could. Give and it shall be given to you.

Country singer Clay Walker sings a great song called, "The Chain of Love". In the song and matching music video, his character Joe stops to help a woman traveler who has a flat tire on the side of the road. After he changes the tire, the woman offers to pay him. He says, "You don't owe me a thing, I've been there too, just don't let the chain of love end with you." The song goes on to tell the story that the woman drives down the road and stops at a roadside café. Her waitress is 8 months pregnant. After eating, the lady hands the waitress a $100 bill to pay her check. When the waitress brings the change back, the woman is gone. The woman had left a note that said, "You don't owe me a thing. I've been there too, just don't let the chain of love end with you." The waitress goes home. Her husband is in bed with his back to her, sleeping. She rubs her husband's shoulder with a look of relief on her face. She whispers, "Everything is going to be all right...Joe." Her husband was Joe. He was the one who changed the flat for the woman by the side of the road.

Don't Let The Chain Of Love End With You

When there are givers, the chain of love will never be broken. The beautiful thing about the "Power of Giving" is that it will come back to you sooner or later. You can use the "Power of Giving" to help you make your vision reality and reach your goals when you give freely. Give your time, volunteer. I said before that volunteering was a great way to meet people and increase your network. Give positive comments to co-workers and others. Pick out positive things about them and let them know. Compliment their appearance (be genuine). Leave them a note on their desk that tells them they did a great job. Give them a card or present for their birthday.

I was talking on the phone to a guy who wanted me to work on a video project. I've known George for a few years and he found out that my birthday was coming up. He sent a cookie jar full of chocolate chip cookies. I love chocolate chip cookies. I worked on his project. How could I say no. George understood the "Power of Giving". It was so nice of him to remember my birthday and it was sincere.

Are you a giver or a taker? The "Power of Giving" will become a lifestyle for you. I am not saying that you have to give everything away; give because you can. Give someone a positive pat on the back tomorrow. It is funny to watch the reactions of students when I speak at schools. I never let a student pass me by in the hall without saying something positive about them like "Cool shirt" or "Great smile" they look at me like "huh?" And then they smile. Not one time have I had a student stop me and say, "Hey dude stop complimenting me." We all like to be complimented. We all deserve to be complimented. Tell those around you that they look great. Tell them that you like their tie, or they did an awesome job, the "Power of Giving" is like magic. When you give from the heart, it will return to you. Give sincere compliments and see if others don't come around you more often and offer to help you when you need it. That's the "Power of Giving".

"Power" Page

Make a list of people you know who could use
a gift from you. Define the gift. Give it.

13
The Three Dangers

Through this book, I have tried to help you to see yourself in a realistic and positive light. I want you to be able to experience the life you have always dreamed of having. I want you to have it all. I really do. I am very passionate about helping you turn your potential into reality. Unfortunately, it does not matter what I want; it matters what you want. You have ultimate control. Nothing saddens me more than to hear someone say, "I want to do this," or "I want to achieve that," and then they don't take real steps to make it happen. Nothing makes me sadder than people whose lives have passed and they have gone to their grave with their dreams, visions and hopes buried with them. Nothing makes me sadder than people who talk a good game and they use every excuse in the book why they couldn't do it. When you listen to those people, it usually turns out to be someone else's fault why they didn't have success. You hear them say, "I couldn't make that sale because our price is just too high," "He wasn't going to buy anyway," "I can't get to the gym today because my favorite show is on."

My question is: Which is more important, working towards your vision of a great, healthy body or sitting on the couch watching a show that you can see later on videotape? That is just a question. You must supply the answer. Too many people are distracted by every little thing that comes along.

Strong People Make Things Happen, Weak Ones Only Talk About It

We talked in the very beginning about crossing the mountains that stand between you and your vision. I told you that the road would take strange twists and turns and there would be dangers along the way. I want to point out some of those dangers in this segment. These dangers are real and can keep you from having the life you want. Being prepared for these dangers will help you overcome them. Danger is seventy-five percent surprise. If you are speeding along a country road and see a sign that indicates a sharp turn, you will have time to slow your speed so that you don't run off of the road. You have avoided danger. If there were no sign or you didn't see the sign, you would only see the sharp turn when you got to it. It would be too late. *Seeing danger too late is what makes it danger.*

You must not fear danger. You must respect danger. I once had a business partner who had some questionable business practices that ended up costing me a great deal of money. Years later I told a friend that I was talking to that former partner. My friend's reaction was, "Why would you talk to that snake?" My response was, "At least I now know that he is a snake." If you are going to handle a rattlesnake, you need to know that there are certain dangers. Being aware of those dangers will reduce the risks of you getting bit.

How you identify and handle danger will increase your odds of making your vision become a reality. Identifying the dangers will put you on a state of alert. After the World Trade Center bombings of September 11th, the United States went on high alert. Be alert for the dangers that can destroy your vision. Just as the tragic events of September 11th happened from within the borders of our great country, sometimes the danger that can destroy you, can come from within as well.

Sometimes dangers such as doubt come from inside of you. Let's examine the most active danger. The danger of doubt.

THE DANGER OF DOUBT:

Doubt comes from within. Doubt can many times be placed in us from other people when we are filled with negative feedback for long periods of time. Doubt ultimately comes from within when we allow it to become a part of our thought process. If others are constantly feeding you negative thoughts and putting down your ideas, you will eventually let doubt occupy your mind and become a part of your very being. That is why we must constantly fill up on positive motivational material. That is why it is so important to praise our children when they do something good, and correct them with a positive touch. I know parents who, in their attempt to correct the child, say some incredibly negative things. I saw a woman in the grocery store the other day. She had a cute little five or maybe six year old boy in tow. The little boy was not all that excited about shopping. Think about it, how many six year olds are? The little boy was climbing on the grocery cart and laying his head on the handle as if he was sleepy. The mother got aggravated and yelled at her very own son, the son that she gave birth to. She said, "Get off this damn cart stupid! Boy you are lazy, now quit leaning on this cart." I was shocked. Here is a little boy who looks up to his mother for everything. He loves her and wants her approval. She should be his hero and role model. He is only six years old and she just called him stupid and lazy. With that kind of reinforcement, what kind of doubts do you think he is going to grow up with?

I deal with young people every day and I can tell you for a fact that they will respond to positive reinforcement a million times better than negative reinforcement. I can go into a school to present an assembly program and build rapport with students and get them to do things that the teacher is amazed by. The teachers always ask, "How come he wouldn't do that for me?" The answer is, people respond to positive, not negative. Negative produces doubt.

You may have grown up in a home where your parents were negative. They probably didn't mean to be, but they were nevertheless. Those years of growing up in that environment may have subconsciously caused the seed of doubt to take root inside of you. Now, when you need to have the confidence it takes to achieve your goals, here comes that demon of doubt that we discussed earlier. If you are fed negative, you will think negative. If you think negative, you will talk negative. If you talk negative, you will talk yourself out of achieving your goals and making your vision a reality. Who do you talk to the most in a day's time? Yourself. You have conversations with yourself in your mind all day, everybody does.

My dad sat me down for a little motivational talk when I was a freshman in high school. My dad was trying his best to get me to understand this concept of positive thinking. As a freshman I wasn't quite on the same page. My dad said, "Son …you are what you think about all day long." This scared me to death. I went around for three weeks thinking I was a girl. What else does a 15 year old think about?

I have a friend who grew up looking for her parent's approval. She, at age 37, now understands that the reason she is so negative and filled with self-doubt is because her parents always pointed out the negative and never the positive. Her father came by her house one day after she had done some lawn work. She had worked long and hard to seed her yard and get it to look nice. I was standing there when she proudly showed him her work. He looked at her work and said, "Your rows are not perpendicular to the house." He didn't say, "Yeah, that is great," or "Good job," he said nothing positive. She really did do a nice job on the yard. It was not important that the rows be perpendicular to the house. My friend was upset about her dad's reaction. She said, "Do you see why I am so negative?"

It is understandable to have doubts. When you have doubts, you must, at some point, realize that those doubts and the negative input are false. You must move beyond what others think. If you don't push through this, you will always be saddled with doubt. There is a way to overcome the danger of doubt. People can only put you down and cause doubts if you let them. You allow them to dump on you by accepting it and then believing it. Exercise the "Power of the Choice." Choose not to accept it or believe it.

Doubt—Don't Accept It And Don't Believe It

THE DANGER OF DISTRACTIONS:

Remember the story I told earlier about the geese? The geese became distracted as they made their way south. Just as with the geese, it is very easy for us to be distracted. Distractions come in all shapes and sizes. Distractions are very tempting and look like good ideas when they are presented. When you are on course to complete tasks that are going to help you move forward with making your vision a reality, you cannot afford to be distracted. A lack of willpower causes the distractions to creep in and become a stumbling block. Your willpower must be stronger than the distraction. There is a great temptation to call in sick or to blow off a half day when your friends call and need a fourth on the golf course. The distraction is not in playing golf. The distraction comes when the golf game is not planned. When the game is planned, it is not a distraction. It is an event that is on your calendar and the time has been allotted. Use the "Power of Time" to your advantage. I am not against playing golf. I love to play golf. In fact, I am a scratch golfer. I hit the ball into the woods and then scratch my head and wonder where it went.

The illustration of the golf game comes back to the "work hard, play hard" philosophy. It may be okay to go play, but if you are going to stay on task, you need to make that time up. Your willpower will keep you on task. Your willpower will be tested early and often when you are trying to achieve something of greatness or value. When you are faced with a distraction, you must combat the distraction with the "Power of the Choice" along with prioritizing. Don't let your lack of willpower change your priorities. It is easy to put something off until tomorrow. Distractions will come and we will give in to them. That is a fact of life. The key is to recognize the distraction and limit it. Don't let it dominate you and your time. Get back on course as soon as possible. If the geese would have stopped at the farmer's pond and only stayed for a day before their journey continued, there would have been no harm. The geese however, let a little distraction become a course-changing distraction. Don't let the distractions that you face change your course and steal your vision.

You Can Stop To Smell The Roses— Just Don't Take Up Gardening

THE DANGER OF DENIAL:
Denial is something that nobody seems to want to talk about. Maybe that is because they are in denial. If we are going to really achieve our desires and make our vision a reality, we need to look at things honestly. If someone smokes three packs of cigarettes a day, they must acknowledge that three packs are a lot before they will seek help to kick the habit. If you smoke three packs a day, that is most definitely a problem. When reaching for your goals, it is vital that you stop from time to time and perform an honest evaluation on yourself. The key word is HONEST.

Denial usually happens when we get ourselves in a situation that we are not proud of or that we know is not good.

A person in denial has a lot of pride and doesn't want to admit that they may be wrong. Don't let your pride become a stumbling block that steals your desires and vision. Pride is a good trait. I have a lot of pride and I hope that you do too. Pride is positive but when it turns to ego or a self-righteous attitude, it becomes a negative. Denial comes from a situation where perhaps we have made a mistake and don't want to admit it. A person in the state of denial typically becomes embarrassed and will then rationalize their situation. When all of the logic has been presented about their situation and they know that they need to change, they still deny the facts. They know they are wrong; they just don't want to admit it. Don't slip into this trap. It is a great danger.

Taking an honest look at yourself and your behaviors is a very healthy strategy. Ask your friends and others close to you what they think of you. Take that feedback and match it against what others say. Be strong. It may not always be good news. If you get three out of five of your friends that tell you your breath smells, you may want to take that information to heart. Evaluate yourself each month or so. Are you happy with how you look? Are you happy with the way you do your job? Are you doing all that you can in your relationships? Asking the questions is the easy part. Answering the questions honestly is the tough part. If you are going to stay out of denial, you need to take inventory and evaluate on a regular basis.

I performed a self-evaluation ten years ago that changed my life. I looked at myself in the mirror, literally, and saw that I was way out of shape and looked older than I was. I looked terrible. I was about to get depressed. I could have denied the reflection in the mirror and told myself that I looked okay for a thirty-two year old man but that would have been a lie. I was thirty-two and looked like I was fifty-two. I had a fat little belly that looked awful. Most people want a six-pack of abs. I had a whole keg. My fat, round little belly didn't match my skinny little arms and my sunken chest. I had to make a change. Now, if someone had said to me, "Wow J.T., you sure are getting fat—you are really out of shape," I might have gotten a little upset and said, "No I'm not." I would have started to be in denial. I might have said, "I'm not out of shape—round is a shape!" Nobody likes to have negative things pointed out to him or her. They would rather discover them themselves. That is why a personal self-evaluation is important. It comes from an open heart and mind that seeks to improve.

Because I did a self-evaluation, it was easier to come to grips with the fact that I was out of shape. I weighed about one hundred and twenty-five pounds. That doesn't sound bad except a hundred of it was around my middle. At five foot four inches, I looked like a bowling pin. I exercised the "Power of the Choice" after my self-evaluation and decided to start lifting weights. If you will remember in the segment on managing change, I said if you are going to start an exercise program, don't jump in all at once. I went to Wal-Mart and bought myself a set of one hundred and ten pound barbells and a weight lifting bench. I thought that if I could stay with it for the summer, I would join a gym. I got on the bench the first day and worked my way up to...SEVENTY POUNDS!!! I bench-pressed seventy pounds a whopping ten times. I stuck with it for the entire summer. I worked my way up to bench-pressing ninety pounds.

I did some consulting for a friend of mine, Phil Bailey and instead of paying me cash he bought me a membership to the local Golds Gym. Phil is a workout fanatic. He looks like a model. I looked like a model too. I was the "before" picture. I walked into the gym the first day and saw this guy who was about my height. He was really built. I told myself right then and there that I wanted a body like that. I now had a vision. There were some huge guys in that gym. You know the kind. They have broad shoulders with muscles on top of muscles.

Some of them were so muscle-bound that they didn't look right. They were steroid users. I did not want to be like that. I wanted to be all-natural. I wanted to change my shape and improve my stamina. Working out has become a part of my life. I work out four to five times a week and have gone from a 125-pound weakling to a 145-pound person who looks younger than forty-three and bench-presses two hundred and fifty pounds. I was at the gym the other night and I made a comment to a guy about my age and he couldn't believe that I was forty-three. He said, "I would have guessed thirty-something." I changed my entire body because I took an honest look at myself and didn't go into denial about what I saw.

Don't Accept Good Enough As Good Enough— Be Committed To Yourself

"Power" Page

List some dangers and distractions that you need to avoid.

14
Conclusion

The climb over the mountain that separates you from your vision is littered with dangers that can cause you harm. The three that we have revealed: the Danger of Doubt, the Danger of Distractions and the Danger of Denial, are the most active dangers. These are the ones that you need to be on alert for. If you are going to PowerAchieve and overcome the obstacles that will come before you, you will need to become very honest with yourself. Being honest with yourself may not be easy. You owe it to yourself to take a look at your life in the privacy of your own mind. Take note of changes you may need to make. Making positive changes will aid you to be in a position to have your desires, as well as helping your vision become a reality. Some people call it soul searching. I call it personal self-evaluation, P.S.E. for short. It is PERSONAL. It is between you and you alone. You can take inventory of where you are and what needs to change, if anything, to get you to the place in your life you want to be. It is about you. It is a SELF-evaluation. Don't lay blame at the feet of others. Your life is ultimately about you. Take responsibility. It is an EVALUATION. Just take a look-see into yourself. You don't have to beat yourself up. Just be honest. Just like an airline pilot checks the navigation charts to make sure they are on course, you need to check to make sure that you are on course with your vision.

Don't Let Your Effort Be Less Than Your Vision

I hope that you have filled your "POWER" PAGES with meaningful thoughts and nuggets of truth. This is your book. It was written for you and about you. Make the ideas in this book personal to you. Somewhere deep inside of you whether you are a millionaire or a person struggling to find the next meal, you have a vision of who you want to be and how you want your life to be. My desire is that, through this book, you have been inspired to turn your "potential" into "reality." It is estimated by scientists that we use less than ten percent of our brainpower. I believe that we use less than ten percent of our potential power. You have so much to give and so much to live for. Life is a series of experiences according to Webster's dictionary. Life is meant to be lived. Live it to the fullest. It is your life and you must take control of the wheel and steer yourself to where you want life to go. Follow your vision. Nothing is too tough for you. There are no mountains that you cannot climb. You now possess the powers to achieve. You can PowerAchieve past all obstacles that stand in your way.

Build a strong foundation to stand on. Have a clear vision. Without a vision, the people will perish. Breathe life into your existence by defining and then pursuing your vision. A vision creates passion, passion creates drive, and drive creates results. Write your vision down. What is your passion? It is not enough to dream of "someday". "Someday" starts with today. The entire world is a stage but this is not dress rehearsal. Life is real. You only get one shot. The curtain has been raised. You are on. You are the star. Dream big and then sharpen those dreams into a vision that you can see in your mind. Visualize in detail. Take time to close your eyes and see the future. Dream in black and white, but visualize in color. Start your journey towards your vision by taking concrete steps to get there. Look to the horizon so that you will keep your head up. Plan the future, but live in the now so that you won't regret the past.

Be creative in the ways you solve problems and overcome obstacles. Use your brainpower to overcome objections and obstacles. Your brain is an amazing thing. Use it. If you will attack the problem with confidence and a positive attitude, you will be able to conquer anything. You are above average. Don't think like the average person. When you are faced with an obstacle, remain calm and be creative. Remember the story of Noah and the ark? Noah had to build an ark that was over four hundred and fifty feet in length. He did not have a Home Depot store to run to. He did not have a power drill and power saw to use. Noah built from creativity and hard work. When you are faced with great odds or a gigantic task, you will have to become a "Noah". Remember, professionals built the Titanic; amateurs built the ark. You don't have to be a professional, just don't be afraid to be creative.

Never give up. No matter what, don't ever give up. Be resilient. There will be opposition. With every opportunity comes opposition. Expect it. It will take courage to get up when life has knocked you down. Have courage. Don't doubt yourself and your abilities. Just as the dancers in the ballet who fell when the fog machine put moisture on the stage, you may be going through a tough time. Because you slip and fall in life, doesn't mean you are less talented. It means you are going through a tough time-period.

Life to me is like a summer storm. A summer day can be beautiful. The sun shines and it is calm until the storm clouds roll in. When the storm clouds roll in, the wind blows and lightning flashes. Thunder explodes and rain falls from the sky in buckets. You take cover and get to a place of safety until the storm moves on. We will experience storms in our life. Some will be worse than others, but they all pass sooner or later. After having experienced two tornados in my life, I can tell you that when the storms blow your house down, there is only one thing to do, rebuild bigger and better. When the storms of life knock you down, there is only one thing to do, rebuild bigger and better. Be resilient. Don't ever give up.

The "Power of You" is perhaps the most important key to success. If you are going to make your desires come true and your vision a reality, you must start with you. You have control. Believe in yourself and your abilities. If you are not happy with your habits, behaviors and actions, make a "you" turn and take control. "You are somebody—God don't make no junk." Replace negative behaviors with positive powers. You were born to live. Live the life you have always wanted.

Build relationships with others. A network of friends will serve you well as you serve them. No person is an island unto himself or herself. Invest in your network by investing in others. The "Power of Others" is essential for your success. We all need to have people in our lives that we can go to for help and advice, as well as do business with. When it seems no one is there, we can always call upon our higher power. Don't neglect the spiritual power that is available to you. So many people think that the spiritual side is about church and changing the outside to look a certain way. That thinking couldn't be further from the truth. The spiritual side is about you and the creator of life having a relationship of peace. Period. Don't neglect it. It is the ultimate "Power".

Exercise the "Power of the Choice." The power to choose is an awesome gift. Little choices make up your life. Be aware that your future will be shaped by the choices you make today. What you choose to do today is important. Don't let bad choices that you have made in the past affect today's choices. Don't let your past make you afraid of your future. Take action on the choices that you make. Choices without action are just good intentions. Light the fuse of action on the dynamite choice that you have made and watch the explosion of greatness happen.

Live in the now. The now is the most powerful dimension of time because things only happen in the now. We can plan, but plans are yet to come. We can look back, but that is history. The now is where it happens. You can make it happen for you—now.

Use the "Power of Time" to your advantage. The meter of life is running. Don't waste the gift of time that the good Lord has given you. Killing time will be suicide as you work to make your visions reality. Time is a powerful tool as you turn your potential into reality. Get the edge by getting out of bed twenty minutes early each day. That "20 minutes to achievement" strategy will add almost four, forty-hour weeks to your year. I hear people say, "I could achieve more if I had more time." Well, here is your chance. I just showed you how to get four extra weeks.

Give. Give because you can. There is power in giving. If there were a room full of takers there would be nothing left after awhile because they took and kept it all. If there was a room full of givers there would always be plenty because they would be giving to each other and spreading the wealth. Use the "Power of Giving" to make your world, the world that you live in, a better place. Give someone a break. Give someone a compliment. Give someone a hand when they need it. Give someone advice when they ask for it. Give someone knowledge by teaching them. Give from your wallet when you see a need. Give someone compassion. Give someone a smile and a kind word. Share a laugh and give someone hope. Whatever you do, don't let the chain of love end with you.

You have the power to achieve your hopes, dreams and vision. You are now in a position to make the life that you have always wanted a reality. It is within your power. You belong to the power that you obey. You can choose to have it all today.

Take action on that choice today. If you don't start today, then when will you start? Commit to yourself right now that you will not allow doubt, distractions and denial to rob your soul of the success that awaits you. You were created for a reason. That reason was to achieve. Don't cheat yourself. Commit to yourself in the privacy of your own mind and the quietness of your heart right now that you will PowerAchieve. You deserve to have a happy, successful life. Today is your day. PowerAchieve today.

A friend sent me a little poem that was penned by W. Heartsill Wilson. It reads:

A Prayer for Today

"This is the beginning of a new day.
God has given me this day to use, as I will. I can waste it…
or I can use it for good, but what I do today is important, because
I am exchanging a day of my life for it. When tomorrow comes,
this day will be gone forever—leaving in its place something
that I have traded for it. I want it to be for gain and not loss;
good and not evil; success and not failure; so that I may not
regret the price that I have paid for it."

I put this poem in my calendar and look at it often. I hope you look at it often as well. I hope that you re-read this book often and that each time that you do, you get something fresh out of it and that it keeps you inspired to turn your *"potential"* into *"reality"*.

15
Weekly Themes

In this chapter, I have included a theme and a coaching thought for each week of the year. Each Monday as you set off for work or wherever the week takes you, turn to this chapter of your POWERACHIEVING book for inspiration. This book is small enough to carry with you. Refer to it often. We are on this journey together. Achievement happens daily on this journey. Enjoy it!

Week One Theme

DON'T DEPEND ON LUCK...IT IS HARD
TO WORK WITH YOUR FINGERS CROSSED.

I have a friend who I drag race with on Saturdays. A few years ago he was racing at our local drag strip in a $10,000 race. Well, lo and behold he won the race and the $10,000 prize money that went with the trophy. When he went home that night, his wife called her brother with the exciting news. Her brother couldn't believe it. He told her that someone from their town had won the lottery that night too. She said, "Well, I better check my ticket." After checking her ticket, she realized that they also won half of twenty million dollars. While this is a great story, it does not happen every day. More people get up and go to work each day than win the lotto. If luck comes your way that is great, but there is no substitute for hard work. Work hard to achieve this week.

Week Two Theme

IF YOU STARE AT THE NEGATIVE,
YOU WILL NEVER SEE THE POSITIVE.

Some people spend so much of their life looking at the glass as half empty they ignore the fact that it is half full and that there is a cool sip of water to be tasted. Some people focus and zone in on every little negative detail of a situation. When that happens, they can't see solutions to the problem. It is almost impossible to solve a problem or overcome an obstacle if you are focused on the negative. Solve problems this week by looking at the positive, creative ways to overcome, rather than staring at the problem itself.

Week Three Theme

MONEY WON'T BUY YOU HAPPINESS— BUT NEITHER WILL POVERTY.

Being happy in life is not about having money, but it sure makes life easier. There will be times in life where you have an excess of money and then there will be times when you will rob Peter to pay Paul because Moses is standing at the door wanting his cash. Having a solid financial plan is key to having the ability to achieve all of your desires. Saving money from your paycheck each week and putting it in a separate account can add up fast. Keeping debt low is important to having financial freedom. If you do not have a financial planner, get one. If you don't know one, call me and I will give a reference (yes, I am accessible). True financial power is not being able to borrow money. True financial power is being able to loan money. Examine your finances this week and get on a plan.

Week Four Theme

YOU CANNOT LOOK BEHIND YOU AND MOVE FORWARD.

The future is where you are going. It is hard to look back and keep a focus on the task in front of you. I was driving through a construction zone one day. It had lots of orange barrels and constant stop, start traffic. Traffic started to move pretty well and as I was moving forward at about 10 miles per hour, I looked in my rear view mirror and saw a friend behind me. I waved to them while looking in the mirror. I looked up just in time to see the car in front of me stopped. I slammed on my breaks and barely got stopped in time. You can't look behind you and move forward. If you are looking behind you, it

111

is hard to see the danger that lies ahead. Many times in life we look into the past and see regrets that hinder any progress we can possibly make. It is okay, and even healthy to reflect on the past, but don't let that reflection take your focus off of the future.

Week Five Theme

STRONG PEOPLE MAKE THINGS HAPPEN; WEAK ONES JUST TALK ABOUT IT.

Talk is cheap. Achieving is priceless. There is something to be said for a man or a woman who says they are going to do something and then actually does it. Most people would rather talk about losing weight instead of actually going on a diet. Most people would rather talk about building wealth rather that to save their money. Committing to your success is easy. Staying with it is hard. Life and most of life's achievements are like running a marathon race. Achieving things in life takes endurance and focus. It is easy to become tired or distracted and quit before the task is complete. Achieving something that you say you are going to do takes guts. If you say you are going to write a book someday, be prepared for the sacrifice of time that it will take to achieve it. Stick with it. People become weary on the journey to achievement. They become weak. You must become strong and use the "Powers" outlined in this book to help you "make it happen".

Week Six Theme

LIFE IS BORING—UNLESS YOU WANT TO WIN.

What makes life exciting? Winning. There is an awesome energy that comes from competing and trying to win. When the competitive juices start flowing, things start getting exciting. There will be adventures while you are competing. In the heat of the battle there will never be a dull moment. Competing as a team or as an individual brings focus and energy that feeds off of itself. There is no time to be depressed. There is no time to take a mental break. There is energy that comes from trying to figure out how to beat the other person. Is your life getting a little boring and stale? Maybe you need to get back into the game and win. Whether you are a sales professional who needs to be rejuvenated to win a sales contest and reach your goal or maybe you want to start your own business, you need to win. Choose something that you desire to win at and go for it. Life is too exciting to be bored.

Week Seven Theme

PRAYER CHANGES THINGS.

When you feel all alone, just remember that there is a higher power that you can talk to. We sometimes neglect a fantastic force that can do tremendous things in our lives. Why is it that people will go see a psychologist but will ignore the creator of the universe? We can have a peace that is so awesome when we just relax in the privacy of our own heart and mind. Develop a time of spiritual prayer and meditation. We all need to have a little quiet time in our lives. This quiet time can be in our car on the way to the office or in the morning when we set aside a few minutes to read something inspirational. I have seen and heard too many stories about the power of prayer to let this super-natural power go unused. I have experienced its power firsthand. It does not matter what faith you are, Jewish, Catholic, Protestant or whatever, it matters that you include this power in your life on a regular basis. Take time to pray.

Week Eight Theme

COURAGE IS BEING SCARED TO DEATH AND SADDLING UP ANYWAY.

We all get scared at some time in our lives. Sometimes we spend a great deal of our time being scared. If we are going to achieve the vision that we have for our lives, we must muster up the courage to go anyway. Firefighters go inside a burning building to save a child. The firefighter is scared to death but understands that there is a job to do. They do it regardless of how scared they are. The same courage that makes the firefighter a hero can be used to help you achieve in your life. Courage comes from within. It is the inner voice that tells you, "Just do it." The fears are real, but so is the power that you have inside of you to overcome fear. The power to saddle up and go anyway will make you a hero in your life. Have courage.

Week Nine Theme

DON'T CONFUSE BUSYNESS WITH BUSINESS.

If you are in business or if you work in a business, there is only one thing that counts—getting the job done. Don't get lulled into thinking that just because you are running here and running there that things are getting done. I was speaking at a school one day and started talking to the janitor. He said, "Do you want to know the secret to being a janitor?" Well, I was not planning a career move but I said, "Okay." He said, "Wherever you go, have a rag in your hand or carry an empty bucket with you. That way they always think that you are doing something." Do you sometimes spend all of your energy trying to fool those around you into thinking that you are really a go-getter? Do you spend all of your time running from one sales call to another? Those around you think, "Boy, old Dave is out on another sales call—that is a hundred this month." But old Dave is so busy running from appointment to appointment that he does not sell anything. You can become so busy running around your office that you think you are busy, but you are not really conducting business. Make sure that you are performing tasks that will make the business grow.

Week Ten Theme

GOD PROMISED TO FEED THE BIRDS, BUT NEVER PROMISED TO DROP THE WORM IN THE NEST.

I was sitting at my desk early one morning when my partner came in. He had this grand idea. We were selling speaking engagements to schools. The strategy that we used was to make contact with the building principal and then send information, which was followed up with another phone call to close the sale. It worked. My partner came into the office and had a new plan. He wanted to do a mass mailing to all of the schools and wait for them to call us. We discussed his strategy for awhile and I tried to convince him that if we did that, we were at the mercy of the mail system. The discussion turned into a heated discussion. My partner who was a church-going man said, "I believe that God will take care of us. He said he would feed the fowl of the air." I looked at my partner and said, "Yes, but he never said he would drop the food into the nest." If you want something you must go get it.

Week Eleven Theme

IF YOU ARE NOT GOING ALL THE WAY, WHY GO AT ALL?

On your journey to achievement, you must resolve within yourself to go all of the way. If you start out on the journey or start to do a task, completing it is paramount. Why do some people spend a lot of time and effort to get halfway complete on a project and then, before it is done, move on to something else? People become distracted or tired and after they have used all of this energy, they quit. Who would plan a vacation to some exotic place, get the airline tickets, pack their suitcase, put a deposit down on the hotel, get to the airport and then decide not to go? If you are going to achieve your vision, you will need to determine that nothing is going to stop you from achieving. Keep going. Do not allow yourself to be sidetracked. Don't spend all of the effort of going part way and then stop. If you are going to go, go all the way!

Week Twelve Theme
KNOWLEDGE IS POWER.

The more that you know about a situation, the more likely you are to succeed. Knowledge is certainly power. If you were in a situation where you were signing a contract, you would want to read all of the fine print or have your attorney look at it. There will be things in that contract that you will need to know because laws, covenants and other language can mean different things than we think sometimes. If you don't know what is in the contract, you open yourself up to danger. When you are in a sales presentation situation, it is important to do fact finding so you will know the needs of the prospect. Without this knowledge you will miss the sale. If you are knowledgeable about real estate and know how to buy properties for no money down, you will be able to make more money than the person that does not know how to do it. If you are going to achieve, it is not only "who" you know, but "what" you know, as well.

Week Thirteen Theme
LEARN HOW TO FEEL JOY.

Joy is a wonderful place to be. When we learn how to experience joy in our lives, we have learned a great secret in achieving. A joyful person is a magnet for others. People want to have joy in their lives and they like to be around those who have it. Joy is happiness kicked up a notch. Learning how to feel joy is not easy. We must quiet ourselves and allow our heart and mind to focus on all of the positive things in our lives. No negative. When we allow ourselves to think on the all of the good and great things in our lives, joy will follow. Feeling joy is one of the most powerful feelings that any person can feel. It is a feeling that bubbles up from the soul and is manifested in a smile and an attitude that allows others to know that there is a hope for tomorrow because there is joy today. Feel joy.

Week Fourteen Theme

IF IT IS NOT IMPORTANT WHO WINS, WHY DO THEY KEEP SCORE?

Keeping score is a measuring stick to see how you are doing in a sporting event. Keeping score in life is important as well. Your "game" may be as a sales professional or a business owner. If you are in sales and you don't keep score of how much you have sold and what the other people in your company have sold, you are missing a great game. It is fun to see how you stack up against others that are doing the exact same task. Selling is like playing golf. You are out on the course with four other people, but you are responsible for hitting your own shots. At games end you will first know how you did by comparing your score against the last time you played and then you will compare your score against the other people in the group. Play within yourself first. Then, compare your "score" against others.

Week Fifteen Theme

THE ONE WHO LEADS GETS THE MOST RESISTANCE.

In stock car racing there is a driving technique that is called "drafting." Drafting is when you follow the car in front of you so close that the air goes over the first car and not the second. When this happens, the first car is getting all of the wind resistance. When you are going 200 miles per hour, the wind is quite strong. The first car is fighting against the wind while the second car has no resistance. Without the wind resistance, the car in second place is actually going faster than the car in front and can pass with ease. The car in front makes it easier for the cars that follow. Being the leader means that you will encounter resistance. Resistance goes along with being a leader. When you encounter resistance from those around you that say, "It can't be done," just remember, you must be leading.

Week Sixteen Theme

GO OUT ON THE LIMB—THAT IS WHERE THE FRUIT IS.

Taking risks are necessary if you are going to achieve the things that you want. You cannot reach an important goal or make your vision a reality without taking some chances. Most people are afraid to go out on a limb because they are not comfortable. When you are trying to achieve anything worth the effort, you are going to have to get comfortable with not being comfortable. If you were on the job the first day as a tree trimmer and were afraid of heights, you would be very uncomfortable. As you got used to climbing the trees, your comfort level would increase along with your confidence. You may never be totally comfortable up in the tree, but that uncomfortable feeling is not the overpowering fear that it was the first day on the job. Little by little you climb higher and reach out further on the limb. You must climb higher and reach further because that is where the fruit is.

Week Seventeen Theme

IF EVERYTHING IS UNDER CONTROL, YOU ARE GOING TOO SLOW.

Pushing the edge is a factor if you are going to achieve the things that you want. Sometimes we get into a comfort zone that does not allow us to push a little harder. We feel that everything is under control. We move along at a comfortable pace and never realize that we must push a little harder and pick up the pace in order to use all of our potential. There is a fine line between being under control and out of control. You must find that fine line in your life that allows you to achieve all that you can and maintain control while pushing to go to the next level.

Week Eighteen Theme

SMOOTH SEAS DO NOT MAKE SKILLFUL SAILORS.

There will be times when the seas of life will toss and turn. The waves of doubt and despair will crash against you with such force that your boat will feel like it is going to capsize. The storms of life will rock your world. You will learn how to navigate the rough seas and how to deal with the mighty winds that threaten to toss you overboard and drown you with fear. You will become skilled at dealing with what life brings because you have learned from life's lessons. You have learned that when a storm comes, it is a test that will help you become more skilled. You will become skilled enough that you can navigate the next storm with ease.

Week Nineteen Theme

WE CANNOT DIRECT THE WIND, BUT WE CAN ADJUST THE SAILS.

When the winds of life threaten to blow us off course, we will have to make adjustments. We can be going through life with such ease, but then the winds of change come and try to take us in a new and different direction. The ability to make the necessary changes that will keep us on course is important if we are going to maintain our heading. We have total control of our ability to adjust and change so that we do not get blown off course and swept into a direction that we did not want to go. We can exercise the power of the choice and make any changes that we find necessary to keep us on course. If we don't adjust our sails, the winds of change will toss us to and fro and we will become an out of control vessel. The control to change course by adjusting the sails is within your power.

Week Twenty Theme

FEAR IS THE DARKROOM FOR DEVELOPING NEGATIVES.

Fear can steal your dreams and keep you from achieving the desires of your life. It is natural to have fear, but if you let fear cause you to become negative, you have lost. Fear can be a motivator. If we are fearful that we will go broke, we will look a little harder for a job. If we are fearful that we are going to be eaten by lion, we will run a little faster. In the jungle the Gazelle is often a target of the lion to become dinner. If the Gazelle wakes up and is negative about the chances of survival that day he will most likely be dinner. If the Gazelle makes fear a positive motivator, he will most likely out run the lion. The mistake that most people make is that they let fear become manifested in negative thoughts and behaviors. Even though you may be fearful, don't let that fear paralyze you with so much negative thought that you can't out run the lion.

Week Twenty-One Theme

WITHOUT A VISION, THE PEOPLE PERISH.

It is impossible to achieve without a vision. "Without a vision the people will perish." That is right out of the Holy Bible. Without a vision of where you are going and what you want to achieve, you will have no chance for survival. You may not physically perish, but inside, you will become as a terminally ill patient. There will be no hope. You will have no life and you will just exist. What do you want to achieve? What do you want to leave as a legacy in this life? Wouldn't it be sad to be an old person and not have taken the opportunity of youth to achieve because there was no clear vision? Find your vision. Live your vision. Make your work on this earth last for generations so that your gift to the world will never perish.

Week Twenty-Two Theme
NO SENSE BEING PESSIMISTIC; IT WOULDN'T WORK ANYWAY.

People who say that it can't be done are right. It can't be done, by them. Why do we listen to people who have no plan? Why do we listen to people who have no vision? If the pessimist is so right, then why is there constant growth in business and inventions? Can you imagine if the pessimist was right; we would still be driving a horse and buggy. Orville and Wilber Wright would never have gotten their little flying machine off of the ground. Henry Ford would never have gotten the automobile rolling. We would still be reading by candlelight because Thomas Edison would never have had an idea that made the light bulb come on. There is a basic flaw in the thinking of a pessimist. Nothing works. If you take a pessimist's point of view, it would mean that there is no sense being pessimistic because it wouldn't work anyway.

Week Twenty-Three Theme
COWBOY UP.

"Cowboy up" is a term used in the rodeo world. It is a term that means to get tough. There are times in our life when we must "Cowboy up." Rodeo is one of the toughest sports in the world. A two hundred pound man gets on an angry two thousand pound bull and will try to stay on and ride the bull for eight seconds. The bull twists and turns and bucks and snorts until the horn blows or the rider is thrown to the ground, whichever comes first. Most of the time, the rider is thrown to the ground first. In life, we sometimes feel like we are on a raging bull that is trying to buck us off. Sometimes life throws us off. We have got to "Cowboy up" and get back on. In the rodeo, some days you stay on the bull and get the prize and some days you hit the dirt, but every day you "Cowboy up". "Cowboy up" this week.

Week Twenty-Four Theme
HAPPINESS COMES TO THE PERSON WHO IS PRODUCING SOMETHING.

Have you ever noticed that when you are bored you are usually unhappy? Boredom sets in and is then followed by its big brother, depression. People are in a positive state of mind and are happy when they are producing or doing something of value. I believe this is why we have an unbroken cycle in poverty and welfare. If a person gets used to not producing anything, they will become bored and depressed and have no ambition. If you are going to achieve your dreams and turn them into a focused vision, you will need to keep working toward producing that vision. Never stop doing something each day that will lead you closer to the ultimate reality. You were designed by the creator to be happy and productive. You will be happy when you are producing.

Week Twenty-Five Theme

IT IS HARD TO MAKE BREAD IF YOU "LOAF".

"Loafing" does not pay much money. I can't remember the last time I saw a job opening that said, "Now hiring - loafer needed". The people that are really bringing home the bread are those who don't. I used to own a bakery and we had our share of loafers. One day, my partner, Rose, was complaining about one of the employees who was just standing around. Helen was standing there gazing off into space like she did most days. Rose said, "Why doesn't she wipe down the counter or something?" I replied that she was earning minimum wage and that she was overpaid. But what did we expect, if she was really a go-getter, she would own the bakery and we would be working for her. Don't let yourself become a loafer no matter what your salary. The only way to make dough is to "RISE" to the top.

Week Twenty-Six Theme

NEVER TRY TO CATCH TWO FROGS WITH ONE HAND.

There is something to be said for focusing in on one task at a time. It is a rare and talented person who can have many things on their plate and achieve all of them at the same time.

It is normal to have many of things going on at one time, but you can truly only give attention to one task at a time. The financial downfall of many companies comes from trying to become all things to all people. If that is your strategy, you will need a great game plan, as well as a great team to pull it off. If you are not focused, it will not work. When you put a magnifying glass over a piece of newspaper and let the sun's rays become focused on the paper, a fire will start. If you move the glass around, the suns rays are never in one spot long enough to become hot enough to start the fire. Focus your energy and start a flame of achievement.

Week Twenty-Seven Theme
GIVE BECAUSE YOU CAN.

It is better to give than to receive. That is true. It is better for everyone involved. It is better for the person who has a need and it is better for the person who has the ability to give. There is something special about giving to someone who is in need. When you give, you are helping to enrich someone else's life. You do not have to just give money, food or clothing. Giving can be manifested in many kind acts that will encourage someone and give them hope. When you give someone hope, you have shown them love. Love is what makes the world go around. Give because you have been blessed. Give because you have the ability and are able. Look around you this week. Who do you see that has a need? Meet that need this week.

Week Twenty-Eight Theme
WHAT GOES AROUND COMES AROUND.

If you are going to achieve all that you desire, you must treat others with respect. It is all too often that people walk over and step on others to climb the ladder of success. When you treat others with little or no respect, it has a way of coming back to you. In the movie, "Hope Floats", Sandra Bullock's character was down on her luck and needed a job. When she came back to her hometown to live, she went to the employment agency to find a job. The woman who was running the employment agency was a girl who Sandra's character had made fun of in school. Needless to say, it was an embarrassing moment when her character was at the mercy of a girl that she once had made fun of. What goes around comes around. Be mindful of how you treat others. You may need their help someday.

Week Twenty-Nine Theme
GIVING UP IS THE ULTIMATE TRAGEDY.

Imagine if someone told you that there was a buried treasure in a certain spot and gave you a map to get there. You would load up the equipment and grab your shovel and go on a treasure hunt. You would be seeking fortune. When you got to the spot indicated on the map, you would start digging. They gave you a map that showed the exact spot that the treasure was located, but they did not tell you how far down you must dig. You would be motivated to dig the first few days. As the days wear on with no sign of a treasure, fatigue sets in. Then doubt sets in. Maybe there is no treasure. You dig a few more days. The hole that you have dug is huge. You are exhausted so you stop digging and give up. Sounds like a logical chain of events. Wouldn't it be tragic if you quit right before you got to the treasure? Don't ever give up.

Week Thirty Theme

YOU ARE WHAT YOU THINK ABOUT ALL DAY LONG.

Your thoughts will carry you to achievement. If you think bad, evil, or negative thoughts all day, then your actions will follow. Putting positive, inspirational thoughts into our mind is a must if we are going to keep our mind cleansed of the negative that comes into our mind. Negative comes from many sources. It comes through the news and others around us. There are many negative sources. We can filter out some thoughts that others try to dump on us. If we allow their thoughts to become our thoughts, then we are not ourselves...we are them. Thinking positive thoughts will clean our mind daily and will be preventative medicine against the deadly disease, N.I.M., "Negative Infection of the Mind".

Week Thirty-One Theme

THE KEY TO A SUCCESSFUL ORGANIZATION IS—
ORGANIZATION.

Being organized is key to being successful and achieving the things you want. There are people who file and then there are people who pile. It does not matter which you are as long as you know where everything is. You may use a hand-held palm pilot or you may still use a day planner. Which keeps you more organized? When you are organized, it is easier to work smarter. When you are organized, you can achieve more and it is easier to work in the "now." Take stock of your organization this week to see if you can become more efficient. It is better to be efficient at a few things than mediocre at many things. Being organized allows you to get more quality tasks done in a less hectic way. Become more organized. That is the key to running a successful organization.

Week Thirty-Two Theme

YOU WILL MISS EVERY GOAL
THAT YOU DON'T SHOOT FOR.

You have got to have goals. Goals are the building blocks that help you live your vision. When I had a vision of writing a book, I had to start by outlining the subject matter and then setting goals of how much to write each day. If I had just had a vision and I had not taken action to set the goals that were needed, I would still just have a vision. Goals are a part of the process of executing the plan. When you plan a trip, you have benchmarks that you want to reach to help you get to your destination. If you were going from New York to Los Angeles, you might have a goal of driving to Indianapolis the first day and to St. Louis the next day and so on until you reach L.A. Without those goals, it would be easy to get off course and just drive around the countryside. The people who are going places have goals.

Week Thirty-Three Theme

IT IS BETTER TO WEAR OUT THAN RUST OUT.

When I traded my last car in, it had over two hundred and fifty thousand miles on it. That car was still a good car. It served me well. It was a beautiful maroon BMW 540. I drove that car hard. Cars are made to be driven. Have you ever noticed how a car can sit in a car lot or in somebody's yard and before you know it the battery is dead and the body is starting to rust? A house that is occupied will sell for more money than a house that is empty. Cars are meant to be driven. Houses are meant to be lived in. You were created to live. If you don't live life to the fullest, then you are not fulfilling your purpose and are wasting your value. Increase your life value. Live every day as if it was your last. So what if you wear out. It is better to have lived and gotten tired than to never have really lived at all.

Week Thirty-Four Theme

LET THE WIND COMB YOUR HAIR ONCE IN AWHILE.

Every once in awhile it is great to just get out and go for a drive. Driving with the top down or sunroof open sets the spirit free. Even driving with the windows rolled down can give you a sense of freedom. I was driving back from Nashville one day when I took the back roads as a short cut. It turned out to be one of my most cherished memories. As I drove through the beautiful rolling countryside, I opened the sunroof to let the heat of the sun warm my soul. I cranked up some of my favorite music as I let my mind clear itself and relax. I allowed myself to enjoy the moment of time and the beauty that surrounded me. We all need to be refreshed. Letting the wind comb our hair every once in awhile is a fantastic way to become free of stress.

Week Thirty-Five Theme

CHANGE THE WAY YOU THINK AND
YOU WILL CHANGE THE WAY YOU LIVE.

Do you sometimes get tired of the way things are going in your life? If so, then you may need to change the way you think about things. Our mind is conditioned to think a certain way based upon our habits. We are conditioned to think that certain things are scary or impossible. If we change our thought process to tell ourselves that it is not scary or impossible, which thought process is correct, the first or second? The answer is the one that you obey. On an episode of the reality show, "Fear Factor", contestants were required to pass three tests to win fifty thousand dollars. The challenges were things like jumping from one moving boat to another moving boat and diving into a pit of rotting squid to retrieve items. Yuk! The last challenge between the two finalists was to climb out on a flagpole 50 stories on top of this building. One contestant kept saying, "I can't do this, I can't do this." The host said, "Yes you can, come on you can do it." She climbed out on the flagpole and retrieved the item and came back to safety. Why was she able to do this? She achieved it because she changed her thinking. She no longer thought she couldn't do it. She changed her thinking and believed that she could. Change the way you think and you will definitely change your life.

Week Thirty-Six Theme

SPEND MORE TIME COUNTING YOUR BLESSINGS THAN ADDING UP YOUR TROUBLES.

It is easy to look at all of the troubles that face us in our life. It is just as easy to look at all of the good things that have happened to us. We have a tendency to focus on the bad and take the good for granted. When you write down all of the problems that you are faced with in the next three or four months, the list will be short when you compare it to a list of the blessings you have received in this life. Do we have troubles in life? Yes we do. If you don't have troubles in life, call me right away so we can market your formula. The troubles seem large, but they are not big at all when you compare them to your blessings. That is why it is important to put things in perspective by spending more time counting your blessings than adding up your troubles.

Week Thirty-Seven Theme

A WALK IS AS GOOD AS A HIT.

When I played baseball as a kid, I would go up to bat and I would always hear the coach yell, "Come on J.T., a walk is as good as a hit." I wanted to get a hit so badly. Because I was so short, the pitcher would always throw the ball high and walk me. I would walk to first base with disappointment that I did not get a hit. I got "another walk." The real fun started when I got to first base. I ran extremely fast. With my speed, I would steal second base. Once I was on second, I would steal third base. The next thing you know, I was scoring on a passed ball or a hit by the next batter. My coach was right; a walk to me was like hitting a triple for anyone else because I ended up on third base. I got to third base because of the opportunity that was afforded me from the walk. When the opportunity arrives, you have to be able to take advantage of it. Not everyone in life is a home run hitter. Sometimes in life you must use speed and skill to score on an opportunity. The key is to make the most of the opportunity. When you do, a walk becomes as good as a hit.

Week Thirty-Eight Theme

YOU DON'T GO THROUGH THE FIRE WITHOUT FEELING THE HEAT .

People who tell you that life is easy are lying. If you are trying to achieve anything of value and substance, there will be difficult and trying times. There will be times that you will feel extreme pressure. Stress will come upon you. You may not be able to sleep. It may cause a hardship. When you go through the fire, there will be heat. There will be flames. It will be hot. You will be tried by fire. Going through this trial by fire will, if you allow it, purify you and make you stronger. We hear stories all of the time about this person or that person going through this great trial and we don't think much about it. However, when we are faced with a great trial, it is different. We now feel the heat. It is real to us. If you want to handle the heat, you must develop an asbestos personality. You must become flame retardant. When you feel the heat, and you will, hang tough. The fire will eventually burn itself out. Don't let the fire cause your dreams to go up in smoke.

Week Thirty-Nine Theme
DON'T LIVE YOUR LIFE WITH REGRETS.

Most people spend their life planning the future and regretting their past. There is nothing sadder than a person who, when at the end of their life, only has a dream of what could have been instead of a memory of what was. When your time to leave this life comes and your life flashes before your eyes, don't you want to see something special? When the curtain comes down on your life and the show is over, you do not want to have missed the second act. Whatever you do in this life, do it with honor and pride before the creator of life. When we live our life to the fullest, we will be able to leave this earth and face our heavenly father like a child who comes home with a perfect score on our test. We are full of pride and have no regrets. We won't be ashamed of what we have done. We have studied and we have passed the test. We have lived life to the fullest and have achieved peace. We have achieved peace because there are no regrets. There are no regrets because we have lived.

Week Forty Theme

THE ROAD OF LIFE IS FULL OF PARKING PLACES.

Every once in awhile you need to stop and fill up your gas tank when you are on a trip. When you are traveling on a long trip, you will stop and eat. On vacation you will most likely visit some exciting places. Life is like a journey. There is so much to see and do. There is also plenty of opportunity to pull off and park. When we pull off and park, we run the risk of never getting started again. Parking is not a bad thing if we know that we are just parking for a little while. The danger of parking on the road of life is when we decide to abandon our journey because we are tired or distracted. On the road of life the people who are going places are moving. Put it in drive and keep moving.

Week Forty-One Theme

DON'T LET YOUR PAST
MAKE YOU AFRAID OF YOUR FUTURE.

We all have a tendency to let our past dictate our future. If you focus on your past failures, you will be handcuffed in the future. If you allow the past failures to dominate your thoughts, you will be afraid to try something new. Your past will have robbed you of your future. When a person gets thrown off of a horse, they say the best thing to do is get back on and try it again. This is a true strategy. If a person gets thrown from a horse and says, "That is it, I will never get on a horse again," that person is cheating themselves of learning to ride a beautiful animal. Because you get turned down for a couple of jobs, does it mean that you stop looking for a job? No. We all get thrown from time to time in life. We can't let that stop us from trying it again in the future. We can't let what has happened in the past make us afraid of trying it again in the future.

Week Forty-Two Theme

SEEING DANGER TOO LATE IS WHAT MAKES IT DANGER.

Imagine that you are hiking on a mountain with steep cliffs and sharp rocks. The risk of a fall off the side of the cliff is reduced to almost nothing when you see that the rocks in front of you are loose and unstable. If you did not see that danger, you may have taken a nasty fall. Because you saw the unstable rocks, there was no real danger to you. If you did not see the loose rocks until you were stepping on them, there would have been trouble. As we climb the mountains in our life, we must be aware of the potential for danger around us. If we use all of our senses, we will see danger quicker. Using the five senses of smell, touch, taste, hearing, and seeing, will help you avoid danger. Be aware of what is going on around you. Look for dangers that affect your life and avoid them. If you become aware, you will be able to stay away from danger.

Week Forty-Three Theme

YOU ARE SOMEBODY—GOD DON'T MAKE NO JUNK.

When you know that you have come from the creator of life, you have to feel special. Why would someone who is created in the image of God doubt his or her abilities? We shouldn't, but many people do. You may not believe that God created man and that is okay. I just don't think that we all came from monkeys. I choose to believe that God created me along with all the things on this beautiful earth. With that thinking, you can see how God does quality work. If God does quality work and I came from God, that must mean that I am quality as well. If I am quality, then I must not be junk. I must be somebody. When we understand that we are special, we have the freedom to live life to the fullest.

Week Forty-Four Theme

EVEN THE LITTLE GUY CAN HIT
A HOME RUN USING THE RIGHT LEVERAGE.

When I read this line in Donald Trump's book, "The Art of the Deal", I understood it completely. In business and in life, leverage is key. When doing tasks as simple as shopping for a new car, leverage is the key. I was involved in a land deal a few years ago. There were four partners in this deal. We owned a piece of land and were going to build a self-serve carwash on it. Two partners ran into financial problems and could not come up with the money for their share. The third partner was so angry with them that he wanted to cause them to go bankrupt by making them stay in our deal. I saw an opportunity to buy them out which would give them relief and cut the pie into two pieces instead of four. They were all for it. They needed the money. The third partner was being stubborn and refusing to agree to the only real solution. After some debate he said, "Absolutely not." I leaned over to him and said, "Fine, then I will buy both of them out and I will

137

own three quarters and you will own one quarter." He saw that he did not have leverage and agreed to go with the plan. Get as much leverage as you can. Leverage will help you achieve.

Week Forty-Five Theme

WHAT DOES NOT INCREASE YOU, WILL DECREASE YOU.

Life is a constant state of motion. You are either growing or dying. To keep from dying as a person, you must strive to continually grow in areas of your personality. Experience as much of life as you can. Fill your mind with good positive thoughts. You must never allow yourself to stop feeling the goodness that life gives. Read positive books. Listen to positive music and positive speakers on tape. Do not allow yourself to put negative thoughts and feelings into your mind. When you start allowing the negative things around you to become a part of you, they will stunt your growth. You will start to die. If a situation is not making you better, then remove it. If you are not growing as a person, then you need to eliminate the negative things that are holding you back. The things that do not increase your growth will cause the opposite effect. They will decrease you. You were born to grow.

Week Forty-Six Theme

WORK LIKE YOU DON'T NEED THE MONEY.

Some people work to live and some people live to work. I want to work like I don't need the money. If you become so into your job, you will become well off on payday. Payday will take care of itself if you develop a passion for what you do. There are plenty of people who work only because they have to put food on the table. If you are going to truly succeed, you must work because you enjoy the job and the people that are around you. If you don't enjoy the job, you will be unhappy and every day that you go to work will be a chore. It makes a difference to a company when one employee won't do anything extra unless they get paid for it and another employee will pitch in anytime. When it comes time for a promotion, the person who pitched in anytime will be at the top of the list.

Week Forty-Seven Theme

WHEN YOU FIND A STUMBLING BLOCK, TURN IT INTO A STEPPING STONE.

Turning the negative into a positive is a beautiful thing. When you realize that you have the power to turn a situation that could have been bad into something that is good, you understand PowerAchieving. There are times in this life when we all stumble and almost fall. The key to not falling is to balance yourself. When you stumble physically, you catch your balance and go on. When you stumble in life, the same principal holds true. Having proper "balance" in our lives will help turn that near fall into a stepping stone to achieving. Check your balance. Is your life in proper balance physically, mentally and spiritually? If you stumble, catch your balance and make it into a stepping stone.

139

Week Forty-Eight Theme

OPPORTUNITIES ARE NEVER LOST— JUST SEIZED BY SOMEONE ELSE.

Opportunities are in front of you. The key thing to keep in mind is that those same opportunities have been or will be in front of others as well. If you are trying out for a sports team or going to a job interview, you must take advantage of that opportunity. If you don't, there will be somebody else behind you that will. When I was in college I studied theater. I once auditioned for a play by doing a funny monologue. The director suggested that I do something serious since it was a serious play. I thought I would do a funny piece anyway. Big mistake. When the casting sheet was posted, my name was not on it. I blew the opportunity by doing the wrong audition piece. Tom Paksitis, a classmate, got the role that I was after. I lost the opportunity and Tom had seized the opportunity to get the role. Take advantage of the opportunities in front of you. If you don't, someone else will.

Week Forty-Nine Theme

LIGHT BEATS DARK EVERY TIME.

There is no darkness that light cannot overcome. If you went into a dark cave with a flashlight, the darkness would become light as soon as you turned the light on. Many people are afraid of the dark. I don't know anyone who is afraid of the light. Positive will overcome negative just like light overcomes dark. If a positive person walks into a room full of negative people, the room will get brighter. You can brighten the dark world around you by being positive. When you feel negative, read or listen to something positive. The positive will shine so bright that the negative will be gone. It is a fact of life. Light beats darkness every time. Be a light to those around you.

Week Fifty Theme

THE MAN ON TOP OF THE MOUNTAIN DID NOT FALL THERE.

People that make it to the top don't get there without a long tough climb. You just don't go out for a little walk and end up on top of the mountain. If you were going to go mountain climbing, you would be prepared. A mountain climber has all sorts of gear that is used to scale rocks and get up steep places on the mountain. You don't see people who climb mountains having their picture taken at the top wearing loafers, Dockers and a polo shirt. You see photos of people on top of the mountain in mountain climbing gear. Climbing a mountain is a long and hard process that demands planning and work. Climbing your mountains in life will also demand planning and work. Without planning and work, you will have a tough time getting to the top. You will not just "fall" to the top. You must climb.

Week Fifty-One Theme

SOME PURSUE HAPPINESS WHILE OTHERS CREATE IT.

You can create happiness wherever you are. So many people try to find happiness in all sorts of vices and pleasures that this world has to offer. People search for something that will make them happy in their relationships and in their careers. People look for happiness at the gaming tables of Las Vegas. It is a tragedy that so many people spend their entire life pursuing happiness when it is within them. True happiness is inside of you. You can create happy times wherever you go and with whatever you do. Sometimes we get so caught up in doing, that we forget to just be. Be still and listen to the birds sing. Be still and watch the sunset fade away. Be still and watch the clouds paint the sky. Be still and love. Love ourselves. Love our mate. Love our friends. Love our creator. Love the world around us. Happiness is not out there somewhere. Happiness is wherever you are. You can create happiness.

Week Fifty-Two Theme

DON'T LET THE PERSON IN THE MIRROR STEAL YOUR DREAMS.

The person who you see every morning in the mirror must be watched. You must keep a close eye on the person in the mirror. If you are not careful, the person in the mirror will convince you that you can't. You can't do this or you can't do that. The biggest dream thief is you. Sometimes we talk ourselves out of doing something because we doubt that we could achieve it. We have this little talk with the person in the mirror and the person in the mirror convinces us that it is impossible. We listen and then allow ourselves to stop pursuing our dreams. When we stop pursuing our dreams, we become only a reflection of who we could really be.

For more information about PowerAchieving visit,
www.powerachievers.com

*To have a PowerAchievers program at your next meeting
or for availabilities and program bookings,
please contact Mr. Stewart at 1-800-379-2871.*